OUR PURPOSES AND WHY?

This is a must read book that could change you for life!

SANDRA A. HURST, RN, BSN

WESTBOW
PRESS
A DIVISION OF THOMAS NELSON

ISBN: 978-1-4497-3777-1 (sc)
ISBN: 978-1-4497-3778-8 (e)

Library of Congress Control Number: 2012901210

WestBow Press books may be ordered through booksellers or by contacting:

WestBow Press
A Division of Thomas Nelson
1663 Liberty Drive
Bloomington, IN 47403
www.westbowpress.com
1-(866) 928-1240

WestBow Press rev. date: 7/02/2012

ABOUT THE AUTHOR

As I, the author, Sandra A. Hurst, RN, BSN is from Detroit, Michigan. A childhood talented fine artist of all types of paints specializing in wildlife and its sceneries. Grew up in a Christian-loving home as the eldest from a family of two sisters and two brothers. As a child, I was always the one who helped my mother cooked and enjoyed it; while my brothers and then one sister played or just simply waited for meals to be ready for consumption. My youngest sister came along when I was eighteen and it was pretty much the same thing of helping my mom cook and now babysitting.

From the time when I was small, snow was never my favorite part of nature. My dream and longing to move some place of a warmer climate constantly remained in my heart. One day, that dream came true from working in a hospital in Michigan that was affiliated with a catholic organization that is established in certain parts of the United States. I was hired at this hospital in 1993 and was able to transfer to Florida to another affiliated hospital in 1995, where Florida has been my home since. After the big move, is when I really discovered more talents than I thought I had. Drawing and painting was one I always had since the age of writing numbers and letters. But after having another dream of reading the whole bible, it was fascinating enough for me to want to write about its contents and what I learned so it could be passed among others.

SANDRA A. HURST, RN, BSN

OUR PURPOSES AND WHY?

Was Adam really the first man?

Illustration by Sandra A. Hurst, RN, BSN

INTRODUCTION

This will help you understand by an introduction of how life began with explanations of spiritual content and the first civilization of man and heritage. Also, explanations of whom may have been the actual first man and why Adam could have not been the first one. The purpose and how evil was formed is implemented from biblical sources. Have you yet figured out why do you and others do certain things without explanation or understanding? Or why humans have negative behavior along with depression, anxiety, abuse drugs or confused about their purpose? This book will explain why God allowed Satan to impose bad experiences and curses upon us and sometimes leads us to unanswered prayers.

There are biblical stories that corresponds with everyday life explained from a point of view of people who lived during biblical times whom experienced the same problems of today. There are also possible biblical proof of reincarnation that will be explained in detail from celestial to terrestrial humans. There are miraculous stories in the bible that can correspond with your faith in God and believing in yourself knowing that you came from Him in heaven and descending to Earth to prove your love to Him. Finally, this book explains some of the values you, your children, and friends will need to make it in life. This book is not intended to persuade a belief or religion. Its sole purpose is understanding the concepts of physical and spiritual realms of nature.

Who was really the first man? And who came to Earth first? Was it really Adam? According to Corinthians 15:45-47, the first man Adam was made a living soul, the last Adam was made as a quickening spirit. If the first man was really Adam, who was the last Adam? Continuing with Corinthians 15: 45, "The first man is of the Earth, earthy; the second man is of the Lord from heaven." God named both men Adam, which means "man". Could the last Adam be Jesus Christ? The last man hasn't been born yet. If you read Genesis 1: 26-28, it says: "And God said let us make man in our image after and our likeness and let them have dominion over other creatures", that are named in Genesis. God blessed them male and female to be fruitful and multiply. But when you read Genesis 2: 4-7, "These are the generations of the heavens and of the Earth when they were created, in the day that the Lord God made the Earth and the heavens."

If Adam was the first man, why would he have generations before him in heaven and the Earth, with him again, being the first? If you are the first man, it wouldn't be generations until you have multiplied from your seed not the seed before you. So, where was this first man exactly created? The bible doesn't say much about where exactly was the first man created. But in the Book of Ezekiel, the Garden of Eden seems to be located in Lebanon. All of this will be explained in further detail. Some areas in the book may be graphic to some readers in regards to sacrificial of animals and the crucifixion of Jesus, and again, this is not to change anyone's beliefs or religion: just only to clarify and to inform. Also, there will be verses and phrases that may repeat, but with different analogies or philosophies.

PREFACE

Everything that happens or happened is for a reason from mistakes to rewards. Mistakes should be treated as rewards and learning tools to help in growth and maturity. One day in Heaven, you were a spirit and God wanted you to come to Earth. In Heaven everything is perfect from personalities to every-lasting love from a Divine Family that never turns its back on you and you not doing the same. Everything happened in Heaven and Earth is for a reason. Before we came to Earth, God knew us and where we were going to spend our temporary home to rectify our soul for corrections and growth. But you said, "wait, I thought everything in Heaven was perfect; so why do we need to come to Earth to rectify imperfections and mature spiritually?" Why would God put us from a perfect world to an imperfect one? This imperfect world brings depression, hate, murder, enemies, greed, stress, death, sickness and many other ill-problems that we have to contend with. Heaven is all holiness and forever glory that is our original and final home after living in this temporary earthly home. We all meant to be in Heaven, this is where our souls originated. God knew us before we appeared on Earth and what our purpose suppose to be. Once the purpose is completed on Earth, we will serve our purpose in Heaven as well. Our heavenly purposes will be different from spirit to spirit likewise as on Earth, where each person serves a different purpose.

After the existence of God, creation began with love and

purpose for all. Good and evil was created along with animals and humans with freewill. Plants, rocks, water and other things of the Earth are of different spirit levels without freewill or instinct. Everything God created is of some sort of spirit, because He is spirit. Though man-made items are not of the spirit, God is still in control of how these things work and will work; because He blessed or cursed the hands that created the things we need or don't need. Spiritual energy is very powerful, and each energy have different strengths from a certain spirit. Everything that God created originated in a spirit form. The universe itself is consist of spirits that are seen(by some people) and unseen. The spirits that are seen by some, enter into temporary bodies that encloses the eternal spirit within. We are as spirits with an enclosed temporary "shell" or body. This book will explain why some spirits enter into temporary bodies and some who never enter them. The spirits that remain outside of a temporary body are responsible for the "enclosed" spirits of the Earth and the rest of the universe. This will be explained in further detail.

TABLE OF CONTENTS

CONTEXT

Depression: Everyone came across it, children and adults. First, it starts with worry and silence. When you don't understand why you don't have or can't have something now, it makes you feel sad and confused along with guilt that can be a part of going through depression. There are chemicals in the brain that are affected when depression sets in. After not being able to figure out the situation or solution to resolve an issue, a chemical is released after long periods of thinking over and over that will eventually leads to a more serious part of depression.

Anxiety: Shortness of breath, tingling hands, worry and diarrhea also is caused by a chemical that's released in the brain, when you constantly worry of how are you going to solve a problem. For example, if I don't have this, I won't be able to do that. Likewise with depression when you are lacking of what makes you happy is when chemicals are released in the brain.

Drugs: The reason people use drugs is to escape the reality of feeling depression and anxiety, it gives a feeling of forgetting everything as if you was dead.

Negativity: When you're depressed or worried, you have a tendency to have negativity. The mind is powerful. Whatever you think or do it comes out into your body and life. We have good and bad hormones in our bodies. Negativity brings out the bad chemicals into your body that makes you ill. These "bad" chemicals are good to a point in order to activate the nervous system in a stressful or an emergency situation, as long as too much is not released. The negative situations like: school, job, marriage, paying bills, or a stressful project that can lead to obsession for perfection, and time of completion can cause feelings of pressure and stress. If there are negative people that bring doubt and lack of confidence towards you, this can lead you to give up. Also, the length of effort without completion and results can cause doubt, making you unsure of yourself. The best way to deal with this is to know your capabilities and your competency. The easiest way to do avoid unnecessary stress is to refrain from things that are out of your reach. Meditate and ask yourself, "will I be able to do this without doing anything else during that time?" Other words, either do one thing at a time or do a minimum amount with the MAXIMUM time allowed. Another example is to use skills, trade or hobbies that's in your greatest strengths; most of these usually come from your childhood.

This will give you a better chance of success and happiness. If you was a child who liked to play doctor, for example, and if this was your favorite game or thing to do even after you grew older, more than likely you may want to become a medical professional. There are adults and children whom experienced certain phenomenon that indicate or reveal a certain purpose. For instance, I saved lives in a few occasions during childhood and adulthood and decided later that I wanted to become a nurse as well as a writer and artist. Have you ever experienced certain things that you ran across in similar, repeating situations? Have you ever been in a fire and survived it many times? Have you been victimized several times and survived it, or saved a victim of crime several times with success? Think very deeply of things that possibly repeats in your life. These repetitions could be revelations of a certain purpose for you. Sometimes you may not experience anything in repetition, but as a child your parent may teach you many things along the way and you either encouraged your parent to constantly teach or guide you into something that interest you deeply, or you may create your interest into a constant hobby or game once you've mastered it. Utilizing all or some of these techniques and experiences can lead to a doubt-free life which can reap less negativity.

Understanding God's purpose: We all were created for a purpose, including animals. In addition, we all were not created spiritually equal, there are different spirit levels that each human possesses that are either considered higher or lower -leveled spirits. We are as angels toward one another and should not envy or hate another, and need to learn to accept that we all are created for a specific purpose. As stated in the bible, God spoke to certain people who wrote the bible, that we all came from heaven as a spirit and became man as Jesus became man also. We suffer because Jesus suffered also, we are all consolations of Him and was created in His image and likeness. As mentioned, this book is not intended to persuade a belief or religion. However, if anyone is interested in sending a question or comment about God's purpose and His existence please feel free to send them. If anyone can create themselves, make the planets spin and remain afloat in a universe that's beyond measure and controls movements of the waters; create things that can be felt or unseen like the wind and microorganisms, please help me understand who else could be this powerful. If anyone who could create themselves they would be too powerful as flesh and blood to begin with. God is the creator with the highest ranks in the Trinity in unity. He wanted to create and send us to Earth and knew our days before and after.

Unity: To be as one from a main source; to be intertwined from a source, one is not without the other; to be connected as a branch from a tree or being part of something that is very similar; and to be as a one.

Reincarnation: Reincarnation simply means to become flesh again, after being from a different body mass (celestial). Becoming flesh is dwelling in a body that is earthbound only (terrestrial); not being able to live in another atmosphere. After we die and pass on into another life to become spiritual or celestial bodies, we leave our remains as flesh here on Earth to turn into dust, and return as spirit or celestial form, being able to live in a different atmosphere where flesh and blood can't. Many people don't believe in this type of cycle. But further explanations will be implemented from biblical principles about life after death and returning to life again from other times on this Earth and from other times from a past Earth. So, is reincarnation possible? Why or why not?

Evil and Satan: Evil is a supernatural force that causes man to sin, and effected other things that were created. Before the fruit was bitten, there was no evil in man. Satan was put in charge to rule evil. Satan's first name was Lucifer, who at that time was an angel of splendid and beauty in Heaven before being overthrown to Earth that brought evil to it. God and his angels fought with Satan in Heaven because he wanted to rule God's throne. But if the origin of evil started with Satan, why was he in Heaven to begin with? Hell is located beneath Heaven with a great gulf fix between both. More details are in chapter two.

First Adam: The first man created whom God breathed His breath of life into the man's nostrils for him to become a living soul, created from the dust of the Earth.

Second Adam: Considered the Son of God name Jesus Christ who was created as a quickening spirit, not being directly from the dust but of spirit that entered as flesh into the womb. The first Adam was not carried by a woman as Jesus was.

Quickening: To be created by conception in a woman's womb in order to be implanted and develop until birth. Before this, a spirit become incarnated at the moment of conception of sperm and egg, as the way Jesus was created, and being born of the Virgin Mary.

Formed: To be created outside of the womb; shaped from matter; to be created and come alive after breath, soul, or electricity is entered or stored into matter. Jesus was not initially considered to be formed but created by entering a womb as a spirit, which was already formed.

Chapter 1

IN THE BEGINNING......

In the beginning, a supernatural being started it all, who is above and controls all things that didn't come on its own account or existence. This Great Celestial Being created everything natural on Earth and in the universe called the heavens. Children, have you ever asked your parents where did babies come from? Your parents should respond to you that babies come from their mothers' womb; which is an organ that holds and nourishes the baby until it's ready to come out. Everyone that comes to Earth has to do this as your parents and their parents had to also. This reproduction started way back to the first man called Adam and the first woman called Eve when they made babies that grew and made more babies. The Supernatural Being who is called God created these two people thousands of years ago near the Garden of Eden.

But there was a time before theirs, when these first two people were created, is when God mysteriously came into existence. Nothing created Him and nothing was before Him, God is the beginning and the end as the Alpha and Omega. God was made from matter that could self-appear that no man was able to name or identify. This unnamed matter would be too powerful to touch, view or to come near to. This is why in the bible it states that man has not seen God and lived. This self-made matter was the major part of God's being, but this was not the only matter that was in God. There are many unnamed materials in the universe that man is still unable to identify today! Even the mystery force of gravity is still being studied! In addition, if you study and look at the table of the elements in chemistry, there are new elements that are still being named, studied, and added. For instance, what is the surface of the universe consist and made of? Where does it end and begin? The bible doesn't speak any of these things and how God came into existence and the matter that He is made of. It does say that He is spirit. God wants to keep how He existed hidden. But in revelation, it states that everything will be revealed at the end of time.

A spirit is consist of a vapor and electricity along with many other chemicals that are found in our bodies, which consist of about over 98% of matter of the universe. God has a spirit that is made from the same matter and elements as our spirits are. Before He came into existence, it had to have been a dark "space" that consisted of nothing. Imagine for a moment that it was no stars, planets, galaxies, heavens, skies, sun or clouds. Then all of a sudden a self-propelling matter appeared. This matter is VERY powerful genetically-scientifically and is more than likely of no form, odorless, and possibly consist of an unusual powerful electro-magnetic gas that can destroy all physical and possibly great parts of spiritual matter if it comes to close to it. This could be the only matter or material that does not exist in terrestrial or even most celestial creatures. God is not consist of flesh and blood, He is only consist of celestial matter along with other powerful elements that are within Him.

These powerful elements are not visible to the physical eyes without them being destroyed. After this self-propelled element existed, this was God himself along with other powerful elements that He's made of. The next possible element that could have been a part of God's development into existence is a water vapor that was produced from the heat of the gas and the surrounding cold, dark environment that turned the unnamed powerful gas into a powerful vapor mix. Just imagine how when you fix something hot or warm and put it in a cool or cold environment like a refrigerator or a cold room, you will see water or moisture appear soon afterwards, and water appears out of nowhere! Because of this mix, other elements could have created more elements; like electricity and light waves from the electricity which could have been the first sounds of roaring thunder from God coming forth into His existence. From the actions of the elements, air could have been formed in the mix of this Great Existence. Air alone is made of many elements like: nitrogen, oxygen, carbon dioxide, argon, neon, helium and some other gases; but the main ones are oxygen and nitrogen, with nitrogen being about 20%. Air is another odorless, tasteless and unseen gas that can only be felt and is another part of God.

Though, as many of the elements that are within God, they are in us also. The water and the gases that make up the air are in us as well as electrons that make up the electricity in God and us. We are made from almost all of the elements in the universe. This includes: iron, sulfur, nitrogen, electricity, water, calcium, copper, and most if not all of the other 113 plus elements that are in God as well. Man and animals are made of elements that identify different species from one to another that come from DNA. All creatures have different elements of DNA that make a living organism possible. Each body part of an organism has a part of DNA that is responsible to produce certain parts or tissues and cells in the organism. For instance, one hair strain is made up of numerous of elements that make this one strain possible like many other parts of our body and spirit. After God came into existence, He more than likely created part of the Trinity with Jesus being first of His creations; and created the Holy Spirit. Once the Trinity was completed, they spoke to one another about the following creations. Everything God created was in spirit form before anything became physical.

The elements of spirits whether these spirits were humans, animals, or other creatures were created first. Once all the needed elements were created, each kind of spirit was of different dimensions and powers. Some of them had powers to control other spirits, there are spirits whose powers were just below God's power; and some also have magical powers. There are spirits that are also too powerful to become physical or carnal to enter a body and this is why some spirits will never become terrestrial beings and just remain celestial beings. There are spirits that can enter a physical body, but can be resurrected when it leaves the body; being resurrected means that when a spirit enters a body, it can leave a body and return to it after a certain period. A type of spirit we have can descend from heaven and into a body, which is not too powerful for this body to contain.

Some spirits may be too powerful to enter a body, but can transform into a weaker state in order for this to take place on Earth. Once our spirit enters a body, it only becomes temporary and the spirit will dwell in a terrestrial body; and once a body dies, the spirit will dwell as a celestial being again. No flesh or bone can be where celestials dwell. Celestials have different elements with some being unknown compare to terrestrials. So, these unknown elements, besides the air, water, and electricity that are in our spirits are in God's spirit as well. However, His spirit has much more powerful elements than ours. There are so many elements that came from water or had been produced by water. Examples of these elements and matter are: calcium, lime, mold, algae, fungus, minerals, and other elements on Earth and in the universe as well. Many of these elements come through soil and water also.

The elements that we are made of are what make up the body. But what about our feelings, the music that plays in our mind, dreams, thoughts and reasons along with daily operations of our bodies? Think about brain mass for a moment, it's flesh that is made up of nerves, chemicals, blood vessels, and other elements. All of these parts work fine until the spirit leaves the body. So, what is a spirit and what it consists to keep our bodies moving and functioning? When you try to figure out how God became who He is, take a look at us; particularly our spirits. It can be defined as: the thinking, motivating, feeling part of man, often distinguish from the body; mind and intelligence.

Now, what is in a spirit to make us do these things? Further definitions is that it also gives life, will, consciousness, thought, and connection to the spiritual world that is separate from physical matter. This complex, eternal and immortal part that's deep within us is a mystery to some people. How can something that is unseen with the naked eye that gives life, thought and will to our body that is unable to survive or thrive without it; is made of something that gives the body the ability to do what it needs to? It would take a deep meditating thought that could answer this question. Just think for a moment, that everything in your body is connected to something in order for the other to work. Your heart doesn't beat on its own account because it belongs to a system that it needs in order for it to beat, which is the central nervous system in the cerebellum area of the brain that eventually travels to the rest of the nervous system. The brain is the main line for your physical body, but again without the spirit it's nothing.

Like other things in life that has connections, your spirit has a connection as well. In the Book of Acts 17:28, it states that we live, move and have our being in God. After He came into existence, the intellectual part of Him came along with the spiritual parts of Him as well. The unknown physical matter that caused God to become in appearance has already been discussed, but what about the matter or chemicals that caused Him to have intellect, feelings, and will? There are certain parts of the brain that controls thinking, emotions, voluntary movements, etc. by different chemicals that are located in different areas. Some of these chemicals are hormones and the others are transmitters of the brain. Chemicals in general are usually made up of different combinations of other elements and other chemicals.

As God was coming into existence, the unnamed supernatural matter possibly could have been the main source of all elements, energies, and chemicals found in us after it mixed with other new components in a new environment. Eventually, those chemicals were passed onto us as part of our development. Our spirits are very much like God's spirit as far as similarities are concerned. However, His spirit is different in other ways also. It has much more power and ability and our spirits are just the branches and offspring of His. This spirit controls our life, feelings, thinking, dreams, and is very complex. This is something that was placed inside of us that never dies, enters its carnal level during conception and leaves the body after it's been injured or ill.

Here's another mystery question: how does a spirit stays in a body without it just randomly exiting? It seems that the only time that a spirit leaves a body is when the body is no longer able to sustains itself. How can the spirit remain in a body even after it's been traumatized or stressed? Is there a connection or certain chemicals that keeps the spirit and body attached before the body is too traumatized to contain a spirit? What causes the spirit to not able to return to a traumatized body once it leaves that body? There could be an answer to these questions if you refer to something called a silver cord. This cord is invisible to the naked eye, which connects the body to its spirit.

The body immediately begins to decay once the spirit departs from it. Until this happens, the body is kept alive and warm while the spirit resides within. Unlike toys and other man-made items, the spirit constantly keeps us alive without replacement of devices to maintain it or recharging it. Once an item's battery (life of the item) is charged or replaced, that item becomes alive again. We have a battery that is eternal compared to a battery that needs to be replaced. Nothing on Earth last forever, but the spirit that's within a body is eternal. What is in a spirit that is not in a body that keeps it eternal that the body lacks? In the law of the universe, things that are unseen are eternal and things that are seen are temporary. Celestial beings have different genetic make ups than that of terrestrial beings. Some things that are unseen are in different atmospheres where earthly time and gravity doesn't exist. Also, there are different worlds in the universe where celestials reside. These different worlds inhibit different powers that operate. The part of heaven that God dwells in is more than likely where His existence appeared from. Not all spirits dwell in this part of heaven, because this area in heaven is so powerful certain spirits may not able to withstand the atmosphere of this highest world in the universe. The Earth's atmosphere is considered one of the lower worlds. Our spirits have been through different worlds. Humans are very unique creatures. Figuring out God's existence is beyond comprehension and understanding will always be a mystery. But we all still have to believe that we didn't create ourselves. If we had this much power, we wouldn't be on Earth; we'll be in a much higher place in the universe where we wouldn't need to be taught or guided to achieve higher knowledge, healings, or plans. There is no way to be able to create oneself without having supernatural powers to begin with.

Every creature has something greater than the other, like a spider that forms a web. Can man do that, though he can make the trains and buildings? Or a bird that makes its nest that doesn't fall apart; a beaver that creates a dam; or something immobile like a plant that has the DNA to bloom flowers or produce fruit, all of which, have spirits as well that never die within them. Everything God creates have the power to create also, even an element such as water; which creates waves, which create movement, which creates a new location, which creates a new environment that creates new life. A bird creates its nest so more generations can create more nests and offspring that will serve their purpose as messengers of God: "Curse not the king, no not in thy thought; and curse not the rich in thy bedchamber: FOR A BIRD of the air shall carry the voice, and that which hath wings shall tell the matter" (Ecclesiastes 10:20). God placed a spirit in each of His creations including the waters and gave a piece of His power to each being that can create or reproduce. After His existence, He knew what He wanted and what was in the future.

Before everything became physical and that is seen in the present was previously in spirit form. God wanted to create a physical world below Him to allow certain spirits to be blessed and given an opportunity to show what a spirit can do in a physical realm of existence as well as being able to return to the original spiritual world. Here is a verse that tells us that man came from Heaven then to Earth: "And NO man hath ascended up to Heaven, but he that CAME DOWN FROM Heaven, even the Son of man which is in Heaven"(Luke 3:13). God created everything out of love and we were placed on Earth to be able to experience love even during the stressful trials of the lower world instead of just staying in Heaven Home to show love towards each other. Though after God created Heaven as our perfect home, He wanted us to dwell in a place where everything could be seen and temporary without perfection, which is the opposite of our Heaven Home in order to strengthen and teach us for a better preparation of an eternal higher level; which will be the next life to come after the return of Jesus Christ. We all were in Heaven, our original home after God's existence. Further understandings of this necessary temporary visit to the physical world will be discussed.

In the beginning God created the heavens, Earth, plants, animals and man. He named the first man 'Adam'(meaning man). God created this man in His own image and likeness, which He told to His fellow creators as being the Son of God, the Holy Spirit and possible other powerful creatures; as all three are represented as the Trinity. When God said, "lets make man in our image and likeness, was He referring to creating Adam? Was Adam really the first man created? According to 1 Corinthians 15: 45-47, the first man Adam was made a living soul; the last Adam was made a quickening spirit. The first man is of the Earth, earthy and the second man is of the Lord from heaven. If the first man was really Adam who was the last Adam? Evidently, the second Adam could have represented Jesus Christ. The Earth is still turning, people are being born everyday, the last man has not yet come.

After God Created the first man, He blessed them male and female to be fruitful and multiply, Genesis 1: 26-28. But when you read Genesis 2:4-7, "these are the generations of the heavens and of the Earth when they were created, in the day that the Lord God made the Earth and the heavens." Apparently, God created(already done) these generations when the heavens and the Earth were created the same day! Please re-read the previous sentence right before this one. Who was the first man, and the first female that was created with the man? And why would he have generations before him in the heavens and the Earth if this was suppose to be Adam? Continuing with Genesis 2: 4-7, "And every plant of the field before it was in the Earth and herb, for the Lord God had not caused it to rain upon the Earth and there was NOT a MAN to till the ground. But remember, God created man in His image and likeness; so where was the first man if it was none to till the ground? Referring back to Genesis 1:27 where it says, "so God created man in his own image male and female", which was done by the 6th day and rested on the 7th day. It continued on to say, "but there went up a mist from the Earth and watered the whole face of the ground and the Lord God formed man of the dust of the ground and breathed into his nostrils the breath of life and man became a living soul." God created beasts after the 7th day from the ground also and named the man Adam, which whom named the beasts of the ground. At that time, God said that it was not good for man to be alone.

Now, back to how God created both Adams along with other types of bodies created. The first man was of the Earth, earthy; which could have been the slowest type of creation compared to how the second Adam was created. The second Adam was created as a quickening spirit, which possibly was a quicker way to create man by having his spirit entering a womb for carnal development. There are other types of bodies as well that have different make-ups of matter that consist of celestial and terrestrial bodies (2nd Corinthians 15: 40). Celestial is defined as being from Heaven, heavenly, or belonging to it. These bodies are either as angels, which are immortal or as planets dwelling throughout the universe that constantly renew themselves. Terrestrial is defined as an inhabitant of Earth, earthy; being created from Earth and its contents; things that are growing on land or in the ground. Another type of body is of the water, or being arboreal. This type of body mass lives, eat and perform other activities in water only.

In Genesis 1:20, ...and God said, let the waters bring forth abundantly the moving creature that hath life. So, did fish actually were brought forth in creation from water like man was brought forth from the dry parts of Earth, while sea life was from the wet parts of the Earth; instead of all creatures of the Earth being from the dry parts of it? It seems to be a mystery that man was created from the ground, but sea life could have not been created from the ground and instead was created from water. The celestials whom are made of eternal matter; terrestrials whom are made of temporary matter from contents of the dry parts of Earth; and the arboreal bodies which are made up of contents from water as being the wet parts of Earth are all different forms of creation from the elements.

When God put the first man of the Earth on it, He made him to name and have dominion over the other creatures. However, in Genesis 2:20 it states that Adam named the beasts of the dry parts of Earth or land; but didn't mentioned him naming species of the sea even though they are terrestrials of the wet parts of the Earth: "And God created great whales....which the waters brought forth abundantly...."(Gen.1:21); the whales were already named before Adam was created. What being named the fish? Was it God who seems to just bring forth all sea life from water comparing to forming man as well as beasts of the dust? Is there a special connection between man and beast since both are from the dust? Humans and animals do have the similar body parts in comparison, such as a vertebra and standing ability, along with breathing to exchange oxygen and CO2. Do fish have a special place in God? The isthmus which is a symbol shaped like a fish that represents Jesus who fed thousands of people with fish could be a divine connection to sea life. Since Jesus was one of God's major co-creators, our Savior, could have named the fish of the sea and bonded a connection somehow.

God not only put man over beast on Earth, but also He granted man higher spiritual eminence over spirits of beasts. As mentioned earlier, there are different types of spirits that possessed different powers. These powers came along with levels of authority and dominion. Of all creatures of the Earth, man has the highest eminence, and dominion over all earthly creatures; whether they are animated or in-animated. The inanimate spirits have the lowest eminence while the animated spirits have higher dominion. The higher the level, the higher ability of connecting with God is achieved along with a level of conscience, will and instinct use of intellect. Spirits that dwell in inanimate creatures and objects like rocks, plants, and water has no ability to think at will or use instinct. They totally depend on God and parts of nature's activities to survive or exist. The higher spirits use will, intellect, and instinct to survive with an ability to connect to God. Man has the highest spiritual connection to God, but what about the lower spirits like the animals? Do they have a divine connection to God? Before these questions can be answered, we need to understand the difference of how animals and humans use instinct and freewill.

Instinct is the inborn-given intellect to different species that use it to their benefit. For instance, a bird need the instinct to make a nest in order to lay eggs; while a fox creates a den for its young; or a cheetah that hunts for its prey to satisfy hunger and to feed its young. Freewill on the other hand, is an ability to make a choice for survival; accomplishing an activity. Man uses freewill more often than animals, while animals use more instincts. Both man and beast have instinct and freewill. Many people believe animals only have instinct, which is not true. Animals as well as man have both instinct and freewill. Instinct is the autonomic natural character that is given by all animated creatures. Examples of instinct is when a creature is hungry it will find something to eat; when a part of the body needs to be scratched it uses nails instead of teeth; chewing food instead of swallowing it whole; to relief oneself; when a creature is in pain it will moan or cry; when something frightens it, it will run or panic; after a baby is born, it will develop a sucking instinct in order to be breastfed; a baby will cry when it first arrive, hungry or in pain; and if a creature is tired and sleepy it will automatically goes to sleep. Examples of freewill including the ones found in animals are: getting up to go to work; decision-making; solving a problem; go up or down a flight of stairs; drive a car or walk; caring for offspring; defend territory; fight or fleet; use of hygiene; mate selection and reproduction.

Though man and animal have both instinct and freewill, both have spirits as well that go to different places after it leaves the body. The spirit of man ascends upward while animal spirits return to the ground and possibly go back to God. Animals' spirits came from Heaven as well as humans'. As it states in Genesis, God blessed man and animal to be fruitful and multiply. God is the head creator who gave all creatures powers to co-create and reproduce. The difference between co-creating and reproduction is that reproduction is when two mates create a copy of their species as offspring from their DNA. Co-creating is helping the creator to produce offspring by will. Creation by quickening is a great part of reproduction. Babies are created by reproduction as well as plants that disperses its seeds on the ground, by which, that same seed reproduced the same plant that dispersed the seed. The difference in creation compare to reproduction is that creation is when the creator used matter of different sources to create the creature or thing. Reproduction is copying from the source, by using the original matter to reproduce by developing the same offspring as the original or parent matter.

All creatures know when it's time for their reproduction. Also, they know other time of events that happen in their lives, as stated in Jeremiah 8:7: "Yea, the stork in the heavens knoweth her appointed times; and the turtle and the crane and the swallow observe the time of their coming; but my people know not the judgment of the Lord"; and this is how animals may somehow have a connection to God as well as man. Adam connected to them after naming them, because God didn't want Adam to be alone. After God created Adam, He didn't want him to be alone just with animals as stated in Genesis. This is when God put the man to sleep to create a companion that can relate to him better than animals could. During his sleep, God removed one of Adam's ribs and closed the flesh there of, to create woman; and Adam said, "therefore shall a man leave his father and his mother, and shall cleave onto his wife and shall be as one flesh" (Gen. 2:24).

Apparently, God and Adam had known each other for awhile before woman was created and spoke with Adam about many things. Woman was not created separately like Adam as the first man was. The first woman was partially reproduced and formed out of the dust. The bible does not state exactly how the woman came about as far as her becoming a living soul by breathing the breath of life into her nostrils or stating that the Earth being a mist that covered the whole ground. Adam had to ask many mysterious questions to God after his awakening. One of those possible questions is that he asked, "what is a mother and a father?" Since he was the first man created, he had to ask God where did he come from and whom were the generations of the heavens and Earth?

Why was woman created from a part of my bone? Although Adam was not made as a quickening spirit from the womb of another woman, Adam's spirit had to come from Heaven as well; but it was entered into his body a different way than the people after Adam. The body of Adam was already fully developed after his creation and God knew Adam's spirit and placed it in his body. Adam named his wife Eve, because it stood for the mother of all the living. God had created beasts in Genesis 1:24 and in 2:19, and the woman's creation was mentioned in Genesis 2:22. Though this is a mystery, it shouldn't be a total surprise; God creates and recreates very often even to this day.

After God created both Adam and Eve, why did He called both of them Adam? In Genesis 5:2 it says: God created male and female, blessed them and called their name Adam. The woman was already named Eve, who was the other Adam in this verse? Could this be other evidence that they were not the first and only people? The first generation mentioned was in Genesis 2:4, which any names weren't mentioned; they were as hosts of the heavens and Earth. How were these generations of Adam created? Were they as quickening spirits or as living souls? In Genesis 2:2, is when God ended His initial creation and rested on the Sabbath Day and kept it holy. However, after Adam was awaken from the creation of Eve, he knew his wife and beget Cain; their first son and the first man to be conceived as a quickening spirit. Another mystery after Cain grew and knew his wife and conceived, where did this woman come from , and from what generation? She was the second woman mentioned in genesis that was not named. She couldn't have been part of Adam's generation because she would have been too old for Cain to begin with. The moment Cain's parents beget him is what started another generation.

Cain's wife had to had a generation of her own, even if she was much older than him; where and when did she come to appeared on Earth? This woman had to come from another generation or came from one of the generations of Heaven and Earth that God mentioned in Genesis 2:4. Her generation had to have been one that was close to Cain's for her to be in close age to him, which means that she had ancestors that could have been before Adam. Cain met his wife in the land of Nod, east of Eden that could have had more people created in the entire Eden area. Even if Cain's wife was created right after Eve, that would have even made her too old for Cain or he may just had a wife that was much, much older than him. Cain himself had to grow old enough to have a woman around his age, which he was created as a quickening spirit that caused him to come as a baby and grew into a man. How was his wife created, was she conceived or created from the ground? If Cain's wife was created from the ground, whom could have been the last one created from the ground? It seems that Adam could have been the only man created from the ground, since he seems to be the first man created and others were created as spirits before or after him.

After Adam and Eve's creation, it seems that the following humans were conceived and created as quickening spirits only. During Cain's generation, La'mech his great, great, great grandson took unto him 2 wives. Their names were Adah and Zillah (Genesis 4:20). Adah bare Jabal who was the father of such that dwelled in tents and had cattle; and his brother's name was Jubal who was the father of all such as to handle the harp and organ. Zillah also bared Tubal-Cain, an instructor of every artificer in brass and iron. These were the generations of Cain that were followed by even more people of his time and place.

Besides the creation of Adam and Eve and their offspring, there could be other strong evidence that Adam could have not been the first man and Eve as being the first woman. In the Book of Proverbs 8:22-36, states that we all were predestined in spirit form descending from Heaven then to Earth. First, in Proverbs 1:20: "Wisdom crieth without, she uttereth her voice in the streets"... Were the streets in Heaven or on Earth? Resuming to Proverbs 8:22 which states: "How long, ye simple ones, will ye love simplicity? And the scorners delight in their scorning, and fools hate knowledge?..." To Whom, where and when Wisdom was speaking these words? And it continued to say: "The Lord possessed me in the beginning of His way, before His works of old. I was set up from everlasting, from the beginning, or ever the Earth was. When there were no depths, I was brought forth, when there were no fountains abounding with water. Before the hills was I brought forth: while as yet He had not made the Earth, nor the fields, nor the highest part of the dust of the world. When He prepared the heavens, I was there. When He set a compass upon the face of the deep, when He established the clouds above... (she must have descended to Earth for Wisdom to say the "clouds above")... when He strengthen the fountains of the deep, when He gave to the sea His decree, that the waters should not pass His commandments; when He appointed the foundations of the Earth. Then I(Wisdom) was by Him as one brought up with Him, and I was daily His delight, rejoicing always before Him, rejoicing in the habitable parts of the Earth, and my delights were with the sons of men" (mankind)....these are the men that could have been before Adam... "now therefore hearken unto me, O ye children. For blessed are they that keep my ways. Hear instruction, and be wise, and refuse it not. Blessed are the men that heareth me, watching daily at my gates, waiting at the posts of my doors, for who so findeth me findeth life, and shall obtain favor of the Lord. But he that sinneth against me, wrongeth his own soul. All they that hate me love death."

Referring back to Genesis 1:26 on God's 5th day of creation, He created man in His image and likeness; male and female. If you read where Wisdom was rejoicing in the habitable part of Earth and her being with the sons of men, signifies that God created other beings before Earth was completed or came into existence. The part of the sentence that states the habitable part of Earth is saying that the Earth was not fully ready to be livable for creatures yet, which had to been before Adam; because Adam was created after the 7th day of creation, everything else on Earth had been created before Adam already. If you refer to the previous paragraph where it has the term "sons of men" usually means mankind particularly of Earth and not in Heaven. The term "Sons of God" usually means angels or other celestials that are very close to God. So, when was Wisdom on Earth? Was it before or after Adam? Who were these sons of men that Wisdom was with in the habitable parts of the Earth? It seems that Wisdom was a female being with great powers and very delightful to God who spent time on Earth as well as Heaven and having many human characteristics.

Somehow, we all were under the presumption that Adam and Eve were the first people besides Wisdom and other beings long before them. In Proverbs 9:1-3, it even states that Wisdom could have been with animals. This is the parable: "Wisdom hath build her house, she hath mingled her wine, she hath also furnished her table, she hath hewn out her 7 pillars, killed her beasts, and sent forth her maidens: she crieth upon the highest places of the city"(What and where was this city?). It seems that Wisdom, this female spiritual human being was mingling with many sons of men along with living life of privileges by having maidens in Her presence. She was with other humans and beasts after God created the habitable parts of Earth that possibly was before Adam and Eve. So, it seems as if it was a lot of activities that occurred on Earth before Adam and Eve's existence. The mystery is that were these sons of men including Wisdom were flesh or spiritual beings who inhabited the Earth? Were they powerful in flesh and blood? Was the Earth in its same location as it is today in the universe? If Wisdom was created before Earth was, it seems that she was apparently created in spirit form.

As mentioned earlier, the Earth is set in a lower world and the lower the atmosphere of a world the weaker the power of its inhabitable beings become. This is why again God dwells in the highest world in order for it to contain Him and the subsequent worlds following it. "...Dwelleth not in temples made with hands..."(Acts 17:24); this is referring to where God lives.

God not only created Wisdom, a powerful female spiritual being who governs her authority over us; but He also created other beings of higher power. Many of these beings were as gods or goddesses of certain things that influence our lives. Gods are considered as supernatural immortal beings of power and are referred to as the "lesser gods." In the Book of Acts 14:8-12: ...."and there sat a certain man at Lystra, impotent in his feet, being a cripple from his mother's womb, who never had walked. The same heard Paul speak (who was Saul miraculously converted and leader of early Christianity)... who steadfastly beholding him and perceiving that he had faith to be healed. Said with a loud voice, stand upright on thy feet, he leaped and walked. When the people saw what Paul had done, they lifted up their voices saying in the speech of Lycaonia, the gods are come down to us in the LIKENESS OF MEN; and they called Barnabas(surname of Joseph who was accompanied by Paul as an apostle), Jupiter, Paul and Mercurius..." Jupiter is defined as a Roman god ruling over other lesser gods and all people. The god Jupiter was named after planet Jupiter by the Romans, because Jupiter represented as the largest planet with many storms; which the Jupiter god performed many times. Juno was a goddess of marriage, queen of the gods, wife of Jupiter and the second highest divinity; also represents as one of the small planets or asteroids which revolve around the sun between the orbits of Mars and Jupiter. In Acts 19:35..."the city of the Ephesians is a worshipper of the great goddess Dianna and of the image which fell down from Jupiter?"....and another god is Mars(god of war). What did it meant in the bible where it states that Paul was on Mars' hill? Paul couldn't have been on Mars if he, in continuance of Acts 17:22 ..."and said,"ye men of Athens, I perceive that in all things ye are too superstitious"".

In Rome mythology, Jupiter had a temple built where worshippers would go. The Greeks believed that these gods lived in an ethereal atmosphere, which is an atmosphere of clouds, mist, glistening and very bright that is invisible for mortal eyes to view. As mentioned, the worlds of the heavens are too powerful for normal view in order to contain the powerful dwellers. These invisible homes consist of burnished gold, chased silver, and gleaming ivory(from elephants?); these were similar to the metals that were in the Garden of Eden. There were other palaces and homes below that housed even the lesser gods and demi-gods(half mortal; half immortal beings). All the planets of the Solar System were named after these gods and goddesses, because of the characteristics of each planet that each of the gods represented. Planets are defined as heavenly bodies with apparent motion as distinguish from the fixed stars including: the sun, moon, Mercury, Venus, Mars, Jupiter and Saturn. Now, any heavenly body that shines, by reflected light and revolves about the sun are the major planets in their order are: Mercury, Venus, Earth(as Gaea),Mars, Jupiter, Neptune, and Pluto. The minor planets are asteroids or planetoids that move in orbits between Mars and Jupiter. The planets as gods are: Jupiter, Venus, Mercury, Mars, Saturn, Uranus(a personification of Heaven, regarded as a husband or son of Gaea named as Earth in English) who was overthrown by his son Saturn: (http://annourbis.com/myths-legends/22381-8_zeus_11___jupiter.html).

When Acts described gods coming down, they had to come down from the heavens; this phrase is usually used after a being comes from Heaven. Planets were not the only objects that represented beings and other creatures. There are certain stars that were created as guides for times and seasons. In Genesis, God said, "let there be lights that will be for signs, seasons, days, and years. The Star of Bethlehem was studied by the Magi as the 3 wise men who acknowledged the coming of the Messiah. We all were created in God's image as well as His son's. He was born under the guidance of His star. Jesus was spirit just like man was before coming to Earth, being first of all creations. Genesis reads, that God started His creation in the heavens, with the sun, moon, stars and planets and other celestial beings. In Colosians 1:13-16: …."translated us into the kingdom of His dear Son: in whom we have redemption through His blood, even the forgiveness of sins. Who is the image of the invisible God and first of all creation of all born creatures: for by Him were all things created that are in Heaven and that are in the Earth; visible and invisible… and He is before all things." This statement also includes that Jesus was created before His guided star. A star is defined as any heavenly body(celestial object) as a planet, meteor, the moon, etc. Referring back to how Jesus' star was named as the Star of Bethlehem along with other star names. Since man was created in God's image and likeness, along with Jesus as being the image of God; we are also born with stars that are named and numbered by God that has a special significance in each of us.

In Psalms 147:4, it states, "He telleth the number of the stars; He calleth them all by their names". So are we connected to a star like Jesus was? What is the purpose of the stars for connection to the terrestrials, as what Jesus became? As mentioned earlier, we are about 98% of the mass of the universe. The element carbon is a great part of nature's matter. According to astronomers, we and the solar system are made of stardust along with other mass of the universe. This is what it meant when Jesus said that we are the "light of the world", and astronomers also researched in the text of the Unas Pyramid (4400 years ago) that we are indeed are connected to the stars; this ancient liturgy is one of Earth's oldest writings that was found. This was a complete religious text carved throughout 5 chambers of the Unas Pyramid. One of the carvings stated that the mother of Isis, "Nut" arches her celestial body as stars in the heavens. Star Sirius is Earth's brightest star and is about the size of it! There are other stars that are about the size of Earth that are called Carbon Stars, perhaps they are mostly made of carbon like rocks, animals, humans and plants are partially made of; things that are made of carbon or consist of it is considered organic, as we are, are considered as an organism. The stars that we see as our planets of the Solar System are considered as "failed stars" that are also called "brown dwarf stars" as being gaseous; mainly of hydrogen and helium; unable to shine compare to other stars that shines very bright (http://2divineways.com/stars/information_on_stars.htm)

There are many, many unexplained phenomenon about stars and its qualities and genetic makeup. However, this explain the reasons why stars that makes up the astrology signs that influence life on Earth and other stars that make up the powerful constellations have powers as well as other celestial beings. It's stated in the bible that every star has its own glory, meaning that all stars are not the same in quality and power.

Before and after the birth of Jesus, His star was with Him. In Matthew 2:2: "...Where is He that is born king of the Jews? For we have seen His star in the east, and are come to worship Him." Also, Matthew 2:9-10: "when they had heard the king, they departed and lo, the star, which they saw in the east, went before them til it came and stood over where the young child was. When they saw the star they rejoiced with exceeding joy." The Star of Bethlehem is defined as a bright star hung over Bethlehem at the birth of Jesus of Nazareth, guiding the Magi to the manger; which were the 3 wise men from the east whom were priests having occult powers. So, when a spirit comes to Earth to become terrestrial that spirit remains connected to the celestial realm. Stars that are connected to terrestrials are connected to assigned spirits even before coming to a terrestrial atmosphere.

The spirit that's within the body is guided by a guiding light, for those who never quite understood what a guiding light was; this is what it is, a star that is connected to you. When God created the stars and said let them be for signs, He was not only referring to times; but also to when and how we were to be born on Earth. Without stars our spirits would not thrive in a body. In comparison to an antenna or a satellite that sends reception and signals to televisions; without these the television will be on, but no reception will come through and connection is lost. Likewise without the star that connects to the soul; while in the body or to the spirit once it leaves the body; the guidance and connection to your inner instinct will be lost, even though you may remain alive like a stationary plant. At the moment of conception, a spirit is entered into the zygote's matter and its star is immediately connected with that spirit. But what about in the case of Adam who was formed out of the ground instead of being created in the womb? How did his star connect to him? The possible answer to this is that when God breathed the breath of life into Adam, his star connected to his soul afterwards.

The breath of life was given by a celestial being who was God that created, counted and named all the stars. Terrestrials are connected through each powerful channel through some sort of celestial being. We are a great part of the universe in matter and in law called "karma", and for everything that is on Earth, seen and unseen; represented as a being or not represented as a being has a spiritual connection behind them. Powerful beings like gods and Jesus were able to convert their bodies into different forms; like in the case in the bible where God Himself changed into a bush to talk to Moses, as well as changing from terrestrial to celestial forms. This could be from the glory and powers of their stars. There are biblical verses that seems to state that the sun(a star) is of Jesus who is the Son of God that's from a parable in John 8:12. There is power behind these heavenly beings that influence and governs all terrestrials of the Earth. It even seems that stars can be spoken to, maybe this is where the phrase, "I wish upon a star" comes from.

If you read Genesis 15:5, where it seems that God instructed Abraham to speak to the stars like: '"Abraham was childless and without heir, and God brought him forth to look upon the heavens and said, "TELL the stars if you are able to list them, and said so shall your seed be also."' Other words, it seems that the same stars that we gazed at throughout our lives are not just hanging bright; but also are alive! So, keep wishing upon your star that you may receive messages or be blessed. Again this writing is not intended to change a belief or religion, it only gives certain facts of why we are here and how we got here. This writing collected facts from biblical statements as well as scientific ones. As mentioned, if man was powerful enough to create oneself on the Earth he stands on, his fellow beings and the atmosphere would not stand. In order to be this intelligent, Earth wouldn't need to be your home whether it's permanent or temporary.

Chapter 2

HE DWELLED IN HEAVEN AND ....THEN EVIL WAS BORN.

Chapter one talked about God's existence and His creations. Everything in Heaven is perfect and without void. There is no pain, suffering, hate, or sadness. God created the heavens and its hosts out of love, which has power. Many people refuse to believe that love has power that affects their body and life. This is how God used much of His power of creation. Heaven would not stand without it, God's love is what makes Heaven perfect. When God said, "let there be" it was strictly out of love. Every being that's in Heaven has love and praises for God. God knew from the beginning to the end of how the heavens were to operate. But one day in Heaven, after God created all of His angels and other beings in Heaven is when one of these angels wanted the whole kingdom of Heaven for himself. He dwelled in Heaven and was a powerful celestial like God, but not equal in power, then evil was born. This angel's name was Lucifer who was one of the most beautiful beings God created as a great authority figure in Heaven in spiritual form. He was another proof of God's created beings before the existence of Adam.

In the Book of Ezekiel it explained how beautiful and powerful Satan was as: "Moreover the word of the LORD came to me: "'Mortal, raise a lamentation over the king of Tyrus, (personification of Satan) and say to him, Thus says the Lord God: "You were the signet of perfection, full of wisdom and perfect in beauty. You were in Eden, the Garden of God; every precious stone was your covering, carnelian, chrysolite, and moonstone, beryl, onyx, and jasper, sapphire, turquoise, and emerald; and worked in gold were your settings and your engravings. On the day that you were created they were prepared.

With an anointed cherub as guardian I placed you; you were on the holy mountain of God; you walked among the stones of fire. You were blameless in your ways from the day that you were created, until iniquity was found in you. In the abundance of your trade you were filled with violence, and you sinned; so I cast you as a profane thing from the mountain of God, and the guardian cherub drove you out from among the stones of fire. Your heart was proud because of your beauty; you corrupted your wisdom for the sake of your splendor. I cast you to the ground; I exposed you before kings, to feast their eyes on you. By the multitude of your iniquities, in the unrighteousness of your trade, you profaned your sanctuaries. So I brought out fire from within you; it consumed you, and I turned you to ashes on the earth in the sight of all who saw you. All who know you among the peoples are appalled at you; you have come to a dreadful end and shall be no more forever" (Ezekiel 28:11-19).

But you said after reading the verses, "I don't see anywhere that mentions Satan or Lucifer who fell from Heaven, it only speaks about the king of Tyrus." There are several verses in the bible that depicts kings, queens, princes, or princesses as mortal and immortal beings, as Jesus is king of kings, and Satan as the king/prince of darkness. After Satan was overthrown, he incarnated as a high authority like Jesus did when He incarnated. There are angels who were sometimes named as high authorities whom acted as political leaders. One of the several verses depicts the Arch Angel Michael as a prince: "...Then he said unto me, fear not, Daniel: for from the first day that thou didst set thine heart to understand, and to chasten thyself before God, thy words were heard, and I am come for thy words. But the prince of the kingdom of Persia withstood me one and 20 days: but, lo, Michael, one of the chief princes came to help me; and I remained there with the kings of Persia"(Daniel 10:12-13).....knowest thou wherefore I come unto thee? And now will I return to fight with the prince of Persia: and when I am gone forth, lo, the prince of Grecia shall come. But I will shew thee that which is noted in the scripture of truth: and there is none that holdeth with me in these things, but Michael your prince"(Daniel 10:20-21). These verses foretell that, instead of mortal beings fighting amongst themselves, it was the immortal beings of good and evil fighting each other while on Earth. So, when the verse in Ezekiel explained about the king of Tyrus, it was referring to Satan. As mentioned, Satan who is like other immortal beings have the power to transfigure, incarnate, or change spirit powers in order to accomplish a plan or task. God destroyed Tyrus because it was so corrupt by Satan's influence that caused the people of Tyrus to worship him.

One source other than the bible depicts Satan's influence as well. The source that used biblical verses to compare and analyze the meaning of scriptures related to Satan's fall indeed was the influence or is the incarnated king of Tyrus, and is depicted as the Anti-Christ, just as Jesus was the incarnated image of God:

"To confirm this even further, consider what we are told next about this king of Tyrus: "Thou art the anointed cherub that covereth; and I have set thee so: thou wast upon the holy mountain of God; thou hast walked up and down in the midst of the stones of fire. Thou wast perfect in thy ways from the day that thou wast created, till iniquity was found in thee"(Ezekiel 28:14-15). How can the king of Tyrus be an anointed cherub, that is, an angel? Could this be saying that Satan at one time hovered over the very Throne of God? Is this why he is so covetous of it? Could this be why both the prince of Tyrus and the son of perdition want to sit in the seat of God? Notice it says that he was upon the holy mountain of God. In previous articles I have amply described how Satan walked within the very Courts of God. And where are those Courts located? In the Holy Mountain of God! And what is that Holy Mountain? Is it Zion? Yes!...but not the physical Zion, but rather the spiritual Zion! It is a mountain where the angel took John to see the Heavenly City of God, New Jerusalem, which also appears to be shaped like a mountain, descending from Heaven... ."(www.endtimeprophecy.net/Articles/satan-02.html).Please visit this web source for further details. Also:www.angelfire.com/mi/dinosaurs/lucifer.html ; and:(www.heavenawaits.wordpress.com/satan-is-king-of-tyre/), or use keyword: "King of Tyre orTyrus".

Of the sources found, the first one makes more sense, that Satan was the anointed cherub that God appointed in Heaven who was in and knew about the Garden of Eden. Tyrus was the old Lebanon region that the bible speaks about the location of the Garden of Eden with the cedar trees, that's explained later in further details. So, could this be where Satan fell on Earth, since Tyrus is located in the Lebanon region of the Garden of Eden, where many activities, and early civilization of this region of Earth occurred, including the creation of Adam? Another verse depicted Lucifer, as Satan had fallen from his pride: "How art thou fallen from heaven, O Lucifer, son of the morning! How art thou cut down to the ground, which didst weaken the nations!"(Isaiah 14:12); As will be mentioned later, Satan's fall tainted the Earth.

In the Book of Revelation starting in Rev. 12:1-17 John wrote about his vision: "....and there appeared a great wonder in Heaven; a woman clothed with the sun and the moon under her feet, and upon her head a crown of 12 stars. Being with child, cried travailing in birth and pained to be delivered. And appeared another wonder in Heaven and behold, a great red dragon, having 7 heads, ten horns and crowns upon his heads; and his tail drew the third part of the stars of Heaven and cast them to Earth: and the dragon stood before the woman which was ready to be delivered, for to devour her child as soon as it was born. She brought forth a man child who was to rule all nations with a rod of iron and her child was caught up with God and to His throne. The woman fled into the wilderness. Where she hath a place prepared of God, that they should feed her 1260 days. And there was war in Heaven, Michael and his angels fought against the dragon. The dragon fought and his angels and prevailed not: Neither was their place found no more in Heaven.

The dragon was cast out, that old serpent called the Devil and Satan which deceiveth the world. He was cast out to Earth and his angels. And I heard a loud voice saying in Heaven, now is come salvation and strength, and the kingdom of our God and the power of His Christ for the accuser of our brethren is cast down, which accused them before our God day and night. And they overcame him by the blood of Lamb and by the word of testimony and they loved not their lives unto death. Therefore rejoice ye heavens and ye that dwell in them..." Satan dwelled in Heaven, was cast out; then evil was born. Revelation 12:12 warns: "woe to the inhibitors of the Earth and of the sea! For the Devil is come down unto you, having great wrath because he knows that he hath but a short time. And when the dragon saw that he was cast unto Earth, he persecuted the woman which brought forth the man child. And to the woman were given 2 wings of a great eagle, that she might fly into the wilderness, into her place...." (Revelation 12).

So, who was this woman? Having a crown of 12 stars with her feet below the moon? Lets go back to Proverbs in chapter 1:20...."Wisdom crieth out, she uttereth her voice in the streets....7:16: by me, princes rule and noble, even all the judges of the Earth. Proverbs 31...the words of king Lemuel, the prophecy that his mother taught him. What my son?...." So who was this woman that John, the writer of Revelation saw in Heaven? It couldn't have been Mary, the mother of Jesus, because Jesus was the first of all creation, first-born of all creatures. Wisdom, possibly being the 2nd or 3rd creature created, was with God as He was creating Earth, and could have delivered a son much later. The name Lemuel means 'belonging to God' in Hebrew, from a source: (http://www.learnthebible.org/king-lemuel.html).

As mentioned earlier, the baby as being the man-child who Satan pursued would rule all the nations, but was caught up with God(belonging to Him) after Satan's casting that was written in Revelation 12. When Satan was cast to Earth how did he knew that in the first place that he only had a short time? What made him think and wanted to take over Heaven? It seemed that when Satan, who was Lucifer in Heaven was evil to begin with. In Revelation 12:10, "...for the accuser of our brethren is cast down, which accused them day and night before God." Now, this happened while he was in Heaven along with being John's vision. So how was it day and night in Heaven? Unless certain parts or levels in Heaven have days and nights, as where Earth orbits, which is considered the lower heavens; because where Jesus and God, along with other powerful immortals dwell, darkness does not exist.

The war that took place must have been in the lower parts of Heaven. Did Satan and his angels planned this war that took place in Heaven? How long Satan was in Heaven before the fight took place? In Revelation 12:9...."that old serpent called the Devil..." Why was he called as being old? Sometimes old can be referred to as something that occurred a very long time ago, and not only as to living a long time. Something like this could have happened in past times. Like the old phrase, "ask this old house", because of the many memories, generations, or families that spent different times under one roof over the years. Satan had determinedly pursued the woman with the 12 stars after giving birth to a child after his casting to Earth. Why was he so determined to persecute this woman with the child and her seed?

Who was created first, her or Satan? Lets refer back to Proverbs 31 where it was left off from "what my son?" And what, the son of my womb? And what the son of my vows? And his mother's words continued through the 31st chapter of Proverbs, the book of the female being, Wisdom.

The Book of Revelation speaks of the past and future times. In Revelation 12:8, it seems to prove of what happened to Satan was the past, before and after being cast to Earth. And King Lemuel, whom may have been the child that was birthed in Heaven; to be the ruler of all nations. Where were these nations though? Even if Adam was the first man, where was this king to rule the nations if Adam was the only man around? Presuming that it could have been other people here before Satan came to Earth. A king wouldn't rule a nation with no people in it. When Satan was cast to Earth, there were people already here. In Rev. 12:12 it reveals that there were inhibitors instead of an inhibitor, "woe unto the inhibitors of the Earth and sea, for Satan has come down." So, if there were inhibitors on Earth before Satan's appearance; who were these people and what type? Were they terrestrial or celestial? How long were they on Earth before Satan was cast down? Was Adam created before or after Satan's fall? What was the timeline between the completion of Earth and after Satan's fall?

In Genesis 1:31: "....and God saw everything that He had made, and behold it was very good; and the evening and morning were the 6th day." Therefore, God wouldn't say after a war in Heaven that it was very good on the 6th day. In addition to this, Adam was created in Gen. 2:7, after God had rested on the 7th day, which could have been the 8th day, or beyond when God created him; which everything was still good, and after that, Satan had fallen to Earth. However, after God rested on the 7th day, where was Satan? During God's creations from day one up to the creation of Adam, everything seemed to be good. So, this is why Satan's fall could have easily been after the 8th day or beyond. It's definitely a strong possibility that Satan and other heavenly hosts were created before Adam, and Satan knew about the Garden of Eden, according to Leviticus 28, before Adam did. More than likely, the Garden of Eden was already created before Adam. The hint is in Genesis 2:8-9: "And the Lord God planted a garden eastward in Eden, and He there put the man whom he had formed." Other supporting evidence was mentioned in Ezekiel 28, of how Satan, as Lucifer was placed in the Garden of Eden, which occurred before the creation of Adam and existence of evil. Adam was an innocent man when he was created, who knew nothing of evil; Eve was created later with the same notion of knowing nothing about evil.

If you refer to Genesis 1:26, where it states that God said: "lets create man in OUR IMAGE, after our LIKENESS…" then comparing another verse from Genesis 3:22 that states that God had said: "'And the Lord God said, "behold, the man is become as one of us, to know good and evil.…"'" is evidence that Adam and Eve were not in the complete likeness of God, because they, before then didn't know about good or evil, and were not considered as being the first humans created compared to the man created in Genesis 1:26; in which, this man was created completely in God's image and likeness! After God placed Adam in the garden, how long was he in the garden before Satan appeared? It continued to state in Genesis: "and out of the ground made the Lord God to grow every tree that is pleasant to sight, and good for food; the tree of life was also in the midst of the garden and the tree of knowledge of good and evil." So, God had to have known about this tree He created, that evil was to come forth from it somehow and there was no mistake made from Him. Another explanation from a verse that evil was actually created: "I form the light, and create darkness: I make peace, and create evil: I, the Lord do all these things"(Isaiah 45:7); God knew that Satan would be overthrown.

Satan was more than likely overthrown sometime after the

8th day of creation, and went to the Garden; since the 1st through the 6th days of creation were good and perfect, and God rested on the 7th. But who or what led Satan there? How did Satan know that Adam and Eve were there? Were they the only two people in the Garden? After God and His angels cast down Satan, he could have used the same power to keep him out of the Garden. But why Satan was able to slip into the Garden with/without God knowing about it? Once Satan appeared into the Garden how did he knew that God had spoken to Adam and Eve about not eating one of the two trees in midst of the Garden and the rest are ok to eat? God had talked with Adam of not eating the tree of knowledge, but there is nothing written that God warned Adam and Eve about Satan may approach the Garden area.

Though, after Satan was cast down, the inhibitors of the Earth were warned of Satan's casting and wrath. But where were Adam and Eve after Satan's fall from Heaven? More than likely, Adam and Eve only knew the Garden of Eden, even while the Earth's geological structure may have been smaller and condensed until the great flood. All of their needs were met while Adam and Eve lived in the Garden, and had no reason to venture elsewhere. And because of the lack of knowledge of good and evil, their freewill was limited. This is why God made sure that they had everything they needed when they were in the Garden. After Satan approached them while in the Garden, Adam and Eve seemed hopeless, because of their lack of knowledge.

God knew exactly what was going on, before and after His creations. There are verses in the bible where it states that nothing passes God's commandments, not even the waters. This is why it could be a possibility that Satan was led into the Garden of Eden. He knew somehow that God had spoken to Adam and Eve and said, "…and he said unto the woman, yea, hath God said, ye shall not eat of every tree in the Garden? (Genesis 3). After they bit the fruit, they became like gods of knowing good and evil. As mentioned, Adam and Eve were created as living souls, not as quickening spirits, with minds of a newborn. When a living soul is entered or breathed into a body like in Adam's case, he was considered innocent and never knew what evil was; like a very small child that is born as a quickening spirit. Adam and Eve never had parents that taught them from right and wrong. God was the parent of both of them, and for some reason kept the knowledge of evil from being revealed to Adam and Eve, who didn't even know that they were naked as like the innocence of a young child. If a young child was born to parents that never taught them right from wrong, they would be just like Adam and Eve to never know about the knowledge of evil, unless it was taught elsewhere. This is why God said, "Behold, the man is become as one of us, to know good and evil: and take also of the tree of life, and eat, and live forever"(Gen. 3:22); which made Adam and Eve to become more the likeness of God and other beings of power.

So, since we were created in God's image and likeness of the first man, who were we? What was our state of mind when we dwelt in Heaven? Did we knew about evil, or did we have freewill to know what was wrong or right? Is this how we were deceived by Lucifer in Heaven? Does freewill involves knowing what is good or evil? More than likely freewill does involves knowing good and evil, otherwise, just knowing good limits the ability of knowing evil and how to handle it. It is the capacity to choose to do good or evil. After the great war in Heaven, all of the hosts(us) and angels whom may not have known evil would have known it after the war, because they all have seen the evil dragon as Satan. If an earthy man like Adam didn't know about evil, heavenly dwellers before Satan's fall more than likely didn't know either. How would a terrestrial know before a celestial?

As mentioned, God inputted spiritual mass and characteristics in everything He created; and yes, even in-animated objects like fruits and rocks. After Eve bit the fruit, the spiritual particles that were in the fruit transmitted into her and the same happened after

Adam bit the fruit also, for both of them to receive knowledge of good and evil.

This spiritual "nourishment" caused this intellect to enter them, because the Earth and its contents had much more power before the fruit was bitten. But after it was bitten, everything on Earth that had spiritual powers diminished drastically, causing only a small amount of power to remain in everything including us and everything that is eaten by us. What type of spirit was in the fruit that was bitten to give 2 people instant knowledge like the gods? As mentioned, a spirit is the intellectual, emotional and thinking part of man, and being created as a living soul more than likely gives only certain spiritual characteristics of man. But the fruit we eat now, gives us physical-mental health and some degree of healing.

But when Adam was created as a living soul, God only gave Adam a part of what a spirit really is without including the extended knowledge of a "true" spirit. This is why Adam may have been created after Satan's fall; otherwise it seemed that he would have learned of God's warning of Satan's fall to Earth in Revelation that included the other inhabitants, and would have known about Satan's evil intentions. So, did Adam knew about the war in Heaven, since he was created, more than likely after Satan's fall? Was there any noise or effects of Earth's atmosphere while the war was going on? How close was the Earth to this part of Heaven where the war took place? The Earth was perfect like Heaven before Satan was cast down. It even seemed that the beings that were here were able to go from Earth to Heaven and vice versa.

If you carefully read about how Wisdom lived on the habitual parts of Earth with her maidens and with the sons of men also in Proverbs 8. These powerful beings were able to see God's throne from Earth. Earth had a very strong and close connection to the heavens while these powerful beings dwelled here. But after Adam and Eve bit the fruit, this caused Earth to lose much of its connection to Heaven and may have caused the powerful beings that resided here to escape corruption of Satan's wrath. After the fruit was bitten, the Earth as well as Adam and Eve's spiritual levels had changed. Their souls as well as their knowledge changed from the innocence of nakedness to the knowledge of evil. Satan's fall had caused the Earth to lose its spiritual level and it fell with Satan. This is why the "veil" that was the connection between Earth and Heaven was closed and the spiritual beings along with other beings before Earth's disconnection left Earth and remained in Heaven; and Adam and Eve remained on Earth without being able to see the heavens, and the veil closed before them; they were more powerful than man today before the fruit was bitten. As mentioned earlier, the Earth was like Heaven; which made everything immortal including Adam and Eve along with possible other dwellers and creatures. After the fruit was bitten, Earth was no longer a place where immortal beings can dwell, and all of these beings ascended back to Heaven after the veil and connection were closed. The bitten fruit affected everything in the universe that was somehow allowed by God. When Adam and Eve were driven from the Garden by a Cherub, because of what they done, the Garden of Eden lost much of its integrity and powers. But where exactly was the Garden located? This was Adam and Eve's home after God created them and put them there, and wherever exactly they were created must have been near the Garden.

In Leviticus 31:3-16, it spoke of the trees in Eden that were in Lebanon: "Behold, the Assyrian was a cedar in Lebanon with fair branches, and with a shadowing shroud, and of an high stature; and his top was among the thick boughs....(5)Therefore his height was exalted above all the trees of the field....(9) I have made him fair by the multitude of his branches: so that ALL the trees of Eden, that were in the Garden of God, envied him. (10)... Because thou hast lifted up thyself in height, and he hath shot up his top among the thick boughs, and his heart is lifted up in his height; (11) I have therefore delivered him into the hand of the mighty one of the heathen......(15).......and I restrained the floods thereof, and the great waters were stayed: and I caused Lebanon to mourn for him, and ALL the trees of the field fainted for him. (16)....when I cast him down to hell with them that descend into the pit: and ALL of Eden, the choice and best of Lebanon, all that drink water, shall be comforted in the nether (lower) parts of the Earth." From what this was saying, it seemed that God destroyed the Garden of Eden because Satan more than likely took over the Garden after the Cherubs who guarded the corrupt Garden temporarily, had left it by the commandment of God. The nether parts of the Earth is where part of hell is located; but how would the trees be comforted if they are in hell? Are there lower and higher parts of hell, just as there are lower and higher parts in Heaven? And the trees were placed in better parts?

So, what was the purpose of evil if everything was perfect including Earth at one time? Why did God allowed Satan to fall all the way from Heaven to Earth to destroy the Garden? The universe is very large and somehow Satan fell directly and only to Earth? Was Hell formed before or after Satan's fall? How was God's relationship between Satan before and after his fall? What was Satan's size or genetic makeup to make him survive the fall to Earth? Especially in the concern of gravity, where and how far Earth was from Heaven if Satan was able to survive the fall? Was it really a physical fall, or a fall from grace? It seemed that Satan was exceptionally large in order for a third of the stars to fall to Earth after Satan's tail cast them; no one can even predict the third of the universe and its trillions of stars. How far was Earth actually from Heaven and how far did Satan fall from it? How close was the Earth to Heaven then and now? Satan had to have been a celestial being for him to be able to live in Heaven; but did his genetic makeup changed after his fall?

It seemed that his physical characteristics changed after God cursed him to crawl on his belly for the remainder of his days.

Was Satan really a serpent before the curse? What caused the snakes after Satan's curse to crawl on their bellies? Was it because Satan's spirit entered a mortal snake and spoke to Adam and Eve just like God turned into a bush and spoke to Moses, and caused the remaining snakes to crawl? Was Satan this powerful at one time? As mentioned, Satan was a beautiful and powerful angel at one time. Though, after his casting to Earth, it seemed that most of his power remained. He could have entered to appear as an innocent snake to approach Adam and Eve, because he may have been too powerful to appear as his original appearance toward them. Since there was no evil in animals as well as reptiles like snakes, Adam and Eve, being innocent, didn't attempt to escape from the snake. This snake must have had extremities and lost them after the curse when God made the snake slithered across the ground and caused future snakes to be the same.

God knew all about this before the foundation of the Earth. So why did He cursed a creature that Satan had entered to begin with? Why was Satan's spirit spared from the curse? Wasn't he the one that entered the snake and spoke with Adam and Eve about the trees in the Garden? Satan couldn't have been a snake while in Heaven if he was considered as a beautiful angel named Lucifer. In Revelation 12:1-17 it seems that Lucifer's named changed to Satan along with his physical appearance that changed to a red dragon. So what did Lucifer really looked like? Where was Satan's exact place in the heavens? Was he really in the same dwelling as God? Since there is more than one heaven, could Satan have traveled to other parts of it or did he just stayed in certain parts of the heavens? What was Satan's job and purpose in the heavens, since they were perfect dwellings? If you read in the previous passage of Ezekiel, it is written that Lucifer/Satan was a cherub, whose job is to guard God's throne. God gave him much power and purpose that needed to be in Heaven; this same powerful spirit is able to enter into other living beings including humans. The snake whether it was mortal or immortal that Satan had entered was different from the snakes of today; like all of the other creatures during the time before the fruit was bitten. God could had cursed the snake to prevent Satan from re-entering another one. So, this leaves you to wonder why did God really caused all of this to happen? What was the purpose of Him to bring evil to a once perfect part of the heavens that is the region of Earth's location? Before Satan arrived to Earth, everything was perfect and good. Just imagine that everything remained good and never died. If everything was perfect we wouldn't have to suffer through everything we come across with. Just imagine things like insects, animals, people, and plants that never died. Before Satan, there was no death of any kind, or sickness on Earth. When you think about how big the Earth would need to be to contain all of the living things that never died, it would more than likely needed to be about the size of Jupiter or larger to contain all things that never died. Also, if there were no Satan or evil, we probably wouldn't pray or praise the Lord as often as needed before evil existed. Before the curse of Adam and Eve, God had taken care of them by providing food and other materials without them having to work for it. But the possible reason for the existence of evil is to force man to pray and work for his food in order to build more faith and trust in God.

Adam and Eve were like babies at one time for their lack of work and innocence. But the Lord wanted Adam and Eve to become more independent and responsible for what they wanted and needed; as with babies who come from their parents as innocent and dependent of their parents until those parents teach and wean the babies into a new life of independence.

If Adam and Eve had remained totally dependent on God for materials that they didn't have to work for, future generations would have been the same way, with a limitation of knowledge and likeness of God. When the bible said, "God made man in His own image and likeness," is saying that God worked to get everything created, so we too have to work to create our own lifestyle and purpose; and as mentioned earlier, Jesus suffered and that's why we suffer as well. Though evil was created for this purpose, Adam and Eve disobeyed God in the Garden, and this is the effects of disobedience of not serving their purpose. When we disobey like Adam and Eve did, curses can come unto our lives as well, as it was in Adam and Eve's case, which is the reason for a difficult life most of the time. But sometimes God allows us to make mistakes to build a stronger faith that can give us another chance. In Adam's case of disobedience that destroyed the Earth, God allowed Satan to influence Adam and Eve to test them.

The purpose of this test is to prove God our limitations and strengths. But why, after being from a perfect place in Heaven, do we have to be tested every moment of each day of our lives? What did we do to deserve this annoyance? What we may think as an annoyance, is actually our blessing for the next life to come. As mentioned, we more than likely, could have been the hosts who hearkened unto Satan's plans before the war broke in Heaven; and this is why for a probable cause God placed upon us blessings and cursing; life and death, to give us free ability to choose. Here's a supporting verse: "I have placed before you life and death, blessing and curse, and you should choose life" (Deuteronomy 30:19).

When the bible speaks of death, it not only speaks of physical death, but eternal death, as being in Hell. Likewise, when it speaks about life, it includes physical and eternal life, as being in Heaven. Many people think after we die this is it, and there is no afterlife. As mentioned earlier, we all came from our Heaven Home. So, since we came from there, did we ever see the great fight that occurred between God, His angels, and Satan? Our spirits are much older than our physical bodies. One clue from the Book of Jeremiah 1:5: "Before I formed thee in the belly I knew thee…." We lived another life in Heaven, and God placed us on Earth. How were we placed? Were we sent or cast here? Were we the ones that listened to Satan's accusations of the brethren that were in heaven that Rev. 12:9 mentioned? Or were we the brethren that were accused by Satan and his angels? After Satan's casting to Earth, one third of the stars fell with him (Rev. 12:4).

As mentioned, everyone is born under and is assigned to a star like Jesus was. So, the third of the stars that fell with Satan, did they belong to us or to the angels that fell with Satan? Is this why the bible speaks of the Redemption, which means to be delivered from sin or being saved from evil; to buy back (as we were bought with a price for Jesus' life); or to recover by payment? We were as a mortgage when a lender gives a loan that has to be repaid. In biblical versions of redemption are in 1 Corinthians 1:30: "But of him are ye in Christ Jesus, who of God is made unto us wisdom, and righteousness, and sanctification, and redemption...." and in Titus 2:13: "Looking for that blessed hope, and the glorious appearing of the great God and our savior Jesus Christ: Who have himself for us, that he might redeem us from all iniquity, and purify unto himself a peculiar people, zealous of good works." The verses are stated that Jesus gave his life for us so we may be redeemed and that He be purified.

As soon as Satan was cast to Earth, the planet's character had changed at that moment from perfection to imperfection, which is sin. Nothing was no longer perfect in animals, man, plants, and everything else that inhibits the Earth, because Satan had tainted it. Because we all were tainted from Satan's fall, we had to be redeemed. Satan's power that was in Heaven remained even after his fall, but some of his power had diminished significantly. Though God had allowed this fall to occur on Earth, NOTHING passes His commandments, not even the waters: "....the waters shall not pass His commandments..." (Proverbs 8:29). If Satan caused man to sin, it was through God's command for it to happen. Everything that happened or will happen is under God's control. But referring back to the question of how did we get here, whether from being cast or sent, we were redeemed for a reason from a sinful decision we made either while we were in Heaven or on Earth after Satan was cast here.

During the Old Testament, sin had to been forgiven by an offer to sacrifice many animals at an altar in front of a priest. Many times people in those days had to sacrifice many animals in one day for atonement of their sins. The sinners had to do to the catching and sacrificing of the animals by gutting, removing, cutting up pieces of the carcass by offering certain parts to the priest like the fat and blood of the animal, and the priest blessed the offering to God. In the Book of Leviticus 6:2-7, (2)"If a soul sin, and commit a trespass against the Lord, and lie unto his neighbour in that which was delivered him to keep, or in fellowship, or in a thing taken away by violence, or hath deceived his neighbour; (3) or have found that which was lost, and lieth concerning it, and sweareth falsely; in any of all these that a man doeth, sinning therein: (4)Then it shall be, because he hath sinned, and is guilty, that he shall restore that which he took violently away, or the thing which he hath deceitfully gotten, or that which was delivered him to keep, or the lost thing which he found: (5) Or all that about which he hath sworn falsely; he shall even restore it in the principal, and shall add the fifth part more thereto, and give it unto him to whom it appertained, in the day of his trespass offering. (6) And he shall bring his trespass offering unto the Lord, a ram without blemish out of the flock, with thy estimation, for a trespass offering, unto the priest. (7) And the priest shall make an atonement for him before the Lord: and it shall be forgiven him for any thing of all that he hath done in trespassing therein."

This commitment went on for many centuries up to the New Testament.

In another part of Leviticus in 8:14-21 the offering for atonement was done in a certain model: (14)"And he brought the bullock for the sin offering: and Aaron and his sons laid their hands upon the head of the bullock for the sin offering. (15) And he slew it; and Moses took the blood, and put it upon the horns of the altar round about with his finger, and purified the altar, and poured the blood at the bottom of the altar, and sanctified it, to make reconciliation upon it. (16) And he took all the fat that was upon the inwards, and the caul(large fatty omentum covering of the intestines of cattle) above the liver, and the two kidneys, and their fat, and Moses burned it upon the altar. (17) But the bullock, and his hide, his flesh, and his dung, he burnt with fire without the camp; as the Lord commanded Moses. (18) And he brought the ram for the burnt offering: and Aaron and his sons laid their hands upon the head of the ram. (19) And he killed it; and Moses sprinkled the blood upon the altar round about. (20) And he cut the ram into pieces; and Moses burnt the head, and the pieces, and the fat. (21) And he washed the inwards and the legs in water; and Moses burnt the whole ram upon the altar: it was a burnt sacrifice for a sweet savour, and an offering made by fire unto the Lord; as the Lord commanded Moses."

Since the dawn of evil and the sins man committed from it, God needed man to sacrifice for Him. There is no doubt that we were the ones that fell with Satan after his casting from Heaven. Satan did not commit this evil alone, he wanted other members to accompany his evil acts. This is why it seemed during the Old Testament, getting into Heaven was more difficult than in the New Testament. Many parts of the Old Testament spoke about death after committing a certain sin, like Leviticus 20:9:"For every one that curseth his father or his mother shall be surely put to death: he hath cursed his father or his mother; his blood shall be upon him", and like Leviticus 20:11: "And the man that lieth with his father's wife hath uncovered his father's nakedness: both of them shall surely be put to death; their blood shall be upon them." The Lord God wanted to show man how serious sin was, and if not repented, the sin will not be forgiven without the use of sacrifice. Before God sent His son Jesus, he wanted man to feel and see what true sacrifice was about before sending His Son to only let man watch Him die for us.

Couldn't you imagine what Moses and other people went through the process of killing an animal by touching the blood, dung, and insides in order to burn them as an offering for the Lord? Do you have anyone in your family or friends that still has to kill for meat? Are they able to withstand the ordeal of seeing the blood and other parts within the carcass? During sacrifices, this had to be done several times everyday; most people had to kill for meat approximately once a day. God commanded for sacrifices of this kind, because He knew many wouldn't want to repeat a sacrifice that would involves spilling of blood, removing and cutting up certain body parts; this doesn't seems to be a fun thing to do day-in and day-out! This makes a person think before committing a sinful act. This is why God accepted Abel's offering over Cain's, because Abel did more work to offer his sacrifice by using an animal of as one of his best selections. While Cain offered the fruits that he tilled the ground from. Cutting and offering up fruit is much less daunting than offering an animal for a sacrifice of sins. After a sacrifice was satisfactory to the Lord, the curse from a sin was removed.

As stated in Leviticus 26, God allows either cursings or blessings among the ones who sinned or had not sinned in order to be redeemed from Satan's fall: (3)"If ye walk in my statutes, and keep my commandments, and do them; (4) then I will give you rain in due season, and the land shall yield her increase, and the trees of the field shall yield their fruit. (5) And your threshing shall reach unto the vintage, and the vintage shall reach unto the sowing time: and ye shall eat your bread to the full, and dwell in your land safely. (6) And I will give peace in the land, and ye shall lie down, and none shall make you afraid: and I will RID EVIL beasts out of the land, neither shall the sword go through your land. (7) And ye shall chase your enemies, and they shall fall before you by the sword. (8) And five of you shall chase an hundred, and an hundred of you shall put ten thousand to flight: and your enemies shall fall before you by the sword......(12) And I will walk with you, and will be your God, and ye shall be my people."

In Leviticus 26, starting at verse 14 it speaks about the curse: "But if ye will not hearken unto me, and will not do all these commandments; (15) And if ye shall despise my statutes, or if your soul abhor my judgments, so that ye will not do all my commandments, but that ye break my covenant: (16) I also will do this unto you; I will even APPOINT over you terror, consumption, and the burning ague, that shall consume the eyes, and cause sorrow of heart: and ye shall sow your seed in vain, for your enemies shall eat it. (17) And I will set my face against you, and ye shall be slain before your enemies: they that hate you shall reign over you; and ye shall flee when none pursueth you. (18) And if ye will not yet for all this hearken unto me, then I will punish you seven times more for your sins..." This is biblical proof that God does allow evil or good to arise in one's life pending on how the life is lived. The terrors and consumptions in one's life are from Satan's permission from God to allow evil and cursing.

But why was a perfect man like Job had every evil thing happened to him? What did Job do to deserve this? This innocent man suffered for years! Job had children, cattle, a house, sacrificed animals, obeyed God and had many friends and family. This is another proof that God allowed Satan to interfere one's life whether sin-free or sin-bound: "Now there was a day when the sons of God came to present themselves before the Lord, and Satan came also among them. (7) And the Lord said unto Satan, Whence cometh thou? Then Satan answered the Lord, and said, from going to and fro in the earth, and from walking up and down in it. (8) And the Lord SAID unto Satan, "Hast thou considered my servant Job, that there is none like him in the earth, a perfect and an upright man, one that feareth God, and escheweth evil?" (9) Then Satan answered the Lord, and said, Doth Job fear God for nought? (10) Hast not thou made an hedge about him, and about his house, and about all that he hath on every side?...(11) But put forth thine hand now, and touch all that he hath, and he will curse thee to thy face. (12) And the Lord SAID: unto Satan, behold, all that he hath is in thy power; only upon himself put not forth thine hand. So Satan went from the presence of the Lord....(14) And there came a messenger unto Job, and said, the oxen were plowing, and the asses feeding beside them: (15) And the Sabeans(ancient inhabitants of the Sheba Kingdom) fell upon them, and took them away...." And there were other things that transpired downhill in Job's life including all of his family that was taken away, and in Job 3:3, Job cursed the day he was born. Here is another, of what seemed that God either SENT or EXORCISED an evil spirit toward someone: "And it came to pass, when the evil spirit from God was upon Saul, that David took an harp, and played with his hand: so Saul was refreshed, and was well, and the evil spirit departed from him" (1 Samuel 16:23).

There is no doubt that since we all came from Heaven, the test could have started there within the time frame of the great war that took place during Satan's fall of grace. God knew and gave permission to Satan to test Job as He did when Adam and Eve were tested. There is NO mistake in God, He knew about each of these tests that occurred in Heaven and on Earth, and God does not change; even while we were tested in Heaven! God knew that Satan was going to turn evil while in Heaven, otherwise He would have destroyed Him if He wanted to. But Satan was spared to test billions in the future. If God wanted to kill Satan at the time he fought in Heaven, Satan would have been destroyed like the sinners He spoke of in Leviticus 20:9-16. Why wouldn't God destroy man whose habitat on Earth was destroyed by Satan's corruption, and destroyed him instead? If God didn't meant for evil to begin, Satan would have been destroyed before falling to Earth and tainting it. We could have been tested like Job when we lived in Heaven before Satan's casting. God probably had asked Satan like He asked him in the Book of Job: "Have you considered my servant...?", and Satan approached us while in spirit form, but we failed, instead of passing the test like Job.

This is why we are and will be called the Redeemed, because after being created to go through Satan's tests, we will be bought back with a price. Just as when man sinned, he had to pay a price with a sacrifice of blood of a fatted animal that was relatively young. Though God did not sin to allow Satan to test and curse man, He allowed tests to come upon man. And if man endures and pass the tests with the freewill (decision) that was given, whether great or small, a reward will be granted in life and in Heaven. The key difference between allowance and sin is that in sin, man disobeyed commandments given by God; and allowance is when one gives permission to another to commit an act. In God's case He wanted to allow Satan to test us, since we more than likely, while in Heaven turned toward Satan when he was in Heaven deceiving many that he was stronger than God and had better ways to run Heaven. Freewill was given to us even while in spirit form in Heaven, we were created in His image and likeness, which includes freewill. Freewill additionally means that we have the decision to think and say about how our lives will be, as when God created the universe and everything that lives within in it, by using His thoughts and words to make this happen.

All of the events that occurred in regards to evil had to happen in order for evil to manifest for the purpose of tests, trials, and tribulations of man's ability to withstand them within his limits. And because of what God did to us through Satan, He himself had to offer a sacrifice that caused man to not having to sacrifice animals any longer. The sacrifice of God was for past and future generations. Even though we turned to Satan's corruption while in Heaven, God loved us then and still loves us now. Through His sacrifice is how we will be redeemed, if we passed and endured all the tests and trials in life, and believing that we were created in His image and likeness, we will have greater rewards and powers in the next life to come. Being in the likeness of God not only mean the characteristics we inherited, but also the things we must do and practice, and God doing the same, such as sacrifice. God must show how much He loves us even in our shortfall of grace by offering a sacrifice, and we must show how much we love Him by offering a sacrifice of prayer and endurance.

Chapter 3

THE ULTIMATE SACRIFICE

Chapter 2 discussed how evil began and the purpose of it. God knew that one day that He had to bring forth evil. Because of the attributes between God and Satan, we were redeemed by an offer of sacrifice from God. Without evil, sacrifice would be impossible, because no man can kill an immortal being. Evil caused mortality to be born, there were no mortal beings before the foundations of evil. Mortality was needed in order to sacrifice, which enabled man to sacrifice animals before Jesus' death, and enabled God to sacrifice His only begotten son Jesus once he became mortal and died on the cross. God offered this sacrifice as a price He paid for what we have to go through with Satan, by allowing tests and trials to be in our lives. Jesus was God's ultimate sacrifice.

In the early days of sacrifice, man had to offer his best sacrifice to God for his sins, which was an animal without blemish, spots, and healthy: just as Jesus was without blemish and sin, whose sacrifice was for man's sin and redemption. As mentioned, we were created in God's image and likeness including being fruitful and multiply, including offering sacrifices. God created an offspring for His sacrifice to be possible. This offspring from God was one of His first creations. This creation was the Son of God who was and still is very powerful like his Father. God's Son, just like us, was in spirit form before becoming mortal. But as mentioned, there are spirits that possess more powers than others. God's Son was created as a High Priest of the most High God, he was not an ordinary man that had a spirit that entered by conception of sperm and ovum of an earthly mother and father. God's Son was mortally created from a different method than of an ordinary mortal man's creation.

When we were created, we possessed a spirit that was suitable to enter into a womb after conception between one man and one woman. But in Jesus' case, his spirit entered into a mortal parent: by an unusual conception between the mortal mother and the Holy Spirit/Ghost to become mortal man. This was not the only time that an immortal being conceived with mortal ones. In Genesis 6:1-2: "And it came to pass, when men began to multiply on the face of the earth, and daughters were born unto them,(2) That the sons of God(angels or other immortal beings) saw the daughters of men that they were fair; and they took them wives of all which they chose." "...There were giants in the earth in those days; and also after that, when the sons of God came in unto the daughters of men, and they bare children to them, the same became mighty men which were of old, men of renown" (famous);(Genesis 6:4).

In other unusual reproductions, there are mortal beings that also create offspring that do not need a male and a female to reproduce. Reproduction can be accomplished by either asexual or sexual methods to produce offspring, even in mortality. Another reproduction type is when cells multiply by a process called fission or mitosis, which splits their DNA to make more cells. But for asexual beings, they possess both male and female organs within the same body. Though he preexisted in spirit form, Jesus' spirit had to enter a mortal being in order to become a mortal being for sacrifice. However, after being created in spirit form, Jesus was not created by two parental beings; he was one of God's first creations: "...the first-born of every creature"...Col.1:15; "And he is BEFORE ALL things"(Col. 1:17). As mentioned, we were created in God's image and likeness to be fruitful and multiply, to produce sons and daughters, who are called sons of men. But sons of God are immortal beings that God created as spirits, whether they were angels or saints.

To be a son of God, he is considered a being without an earthly father or mother of normal reproduction. In Hebrews 7:3, "without father, without mother, without descent, having neither beginning of days, nor end of life; but made like unto the son of God; abideth a priest continually." So, this proves that Jesus had preexisted before becoming mortal, he lives forever and ever! The purpose of a High Priest of the Most High God is to offer gifts and sacrifices for sins: "For every high priest taken from among men is ordained for men in things pertaining to God, that he may offer both gifts and sacrifices for sins" (Hebrews 5). Though Jesus lives forever, he was commanded by his Father, God, one day while in Heaven to become mortal in order for Me to sacrifice you; My Son, for the sins of mortal man that I have caused by Satan's fall. God said to His son Jesus that He wanted man to be redeemed from Satan's transgressions.

God told Jesus that man had to sacrifice animals in order for their sins to be forgiven by a priest, and the priest prays to God for the sin to be atoned. But God wanted to offer more to man for what he had to endure through Satan. As mentioned, God allowed and commanded man to sacrifice animals instead of sending Jesus in the first place; because He wanted man to see what was the true aspects of sacrifice by shedding animals' blood, cutting up the carcass to offer the choice parts to God several times a day was like, which could have been agonizing to see what the animal went through. God also had agonized seeing His own son being sacrificed. The task of sacrificing animals didn't seemed to be a fun task to do that was repetitive several times a day, or every time a sin was committed! When God had chosen His own Son for sacrifice, it was ordained for Jesus to endure the abuse of teasing, beating, physical and emotional pain, betrayal, and unbelief from many that He was the Son of the most High God, even after His preaching. However, when man sacrificed animals, the animal didn't have to endure the continuing physical and emotional abuse of what Jesus went through. The animal only went through a brief physical pain, and by the time the blood was shed, it was already dead.

So, can you imagine what God's emotions was like after sacrificing His son? But God wanted to use His son not only to sacrifice for man, but also to build man's faith, that Jesus can do much more than a sacrificed animal could ever do. Jesus, a High Priest of the Most High God possesses powers for prayers to be answered, performs miracles, and blessed man for those who believed in him by faith that no animal could ever do. Since man had dominance over animals, God used His son as the dominance of sacrifices. In addition, since man had to sacrifice, God wanted to show man that He needed to sacrifice as well; and that man had no preeminence over His sacrifice. What would it look like, after God commanded man to sacrifice animals, and commanded Abraham to nearly sacrifice his own son Isaac, but wouldn't sacrifice His own if we were created in His likeness? Just as Abraham proved his love to God, God proved His love for us by sacrificing His son.

Once Jesus became mortal, according to Matthew 1:1-2, his generation were the descendants of Abraham and David: "The book of the generation of Jesus Christ, the Son of David, the son of Abraham". (2) "Abraham begat Isaac; and Isaac begat Jacob; and Jacob begat Judas and his brethren…" As mentioned, Jesus was mortally born of one mortal parent, of a woman named Mary, and of an immortal parent, which was the Holy Ghost that is explained in Matthew 1:18. Joseph, Mary's husband didn't understand how did this happened with a child being born without his intervention of conception. In Matthew 1:19, it explained that an angel of the

Lord appeared to Joseph in a dream; explaining that it was the Holy Ghost who conceived in her, and not another man. The Holy Ghost chose Mary as being the mortal mother of Jesus, she was a virgin who was a godly woman. With immortal beings conceiving with mortal ones are a part of Greek mythology of how the lesser gods were mighty men of power. Moreover, after the angel of the Lord appeared to Joseph, the angel explained to him that there will be a child born and he shall be called Jesus who will save his people from sins in Matthew 1:21; Joseph listened and remained with Mary. After Jesus' birth in Bethlehem of Judaea as King of the Jews, King Herod wanted to speak with the wise men who have been watching the Star of Bethlehem, which followed Jesus and stood over Him. King Herod wanted to worship Jesus. When the wise men found Jesus, they worshipped Him, offered gifts, gold, frankincense, and myrrh. The wise men were warned by God in a dream to not to return to Herod with Jesus, but instead, they fled into Egypt until the king died; because King Herod would destroy Jesus.

While King Herod was alive, he saw that the wise men never returned and was very angry. In his anger, he ordered to have all children 2 and under to be killed. After King Herod died, an angel of the Lord appeared again to Joseph while in Egypt, and ordered Joseph to go to Israel. But after coming to Israel, Joseph knew that King Herod's son reigned over Judaea, he was afraid of being seen and went through Galilee, and dwelled in Nazareth, and Jesus was called a Nazarene (Matthew 2).

As Jesus grew older, he preached and chose 12 disciples to follow Him to spread the gospel. The twelve disciples were: (1) Simon(who Jesus named Peter), (2)Andrew(his brother), (3)James, (4)John(his brother), (5)Philip, (6)Bartholomew, (7)Thomas, (8) Matthew, (9) James, (10)Lebbaeus, whose surname is Thaddaeus; (11) Simon, the Canaanite, and (12)Judas Iscariot, the betrayer of Jesus. These individuals were not only Jesus' disciples, but also His friends. They followed Jesus as He performed miracles and preaching the word. One may think how can someone, who became from being immortal to mortal and retained all of their powers? Jesus was able to turn water into wine; walk on the water; turn a few fish into thousands to feed the hungry; replaced a man's ear during His betrayal; raised the dead; cast out a demon-possessed man that caused the demons to go into the swine; healed a leper; calmed the winds; cured the blind, and more! Jesus' earthly position as a carpenter was what many mortal men are today. So, how did He performed all these miracles from just being a mortal man?

Though Jesus was the Son of God, even in mortality, His power was influenced by His Father. Here is a clue from a verse in regards to Jesus and his power from God, His Father: "The Spirit of the Lord is upon me, because he hath anointed me to preach the gospel to the poor; he hath sent me to heal the broken hearted, to preach deliverance to the captives, and recovering of sight to the blind, to set at liberty them that are bruised....."(Luke 4:18). In Matthew 10:8, Jesus instructed His disciples to: "heal the sick, cleanse the lepers, raise the dead, cast out devils...." The disciples were able to do these things, because they were chosen and anointed by God through their faith and belief in Jesus. Another verse in regards to Jesus' powers coming from His Father is in John 5:19,...."Verily, verily, I say unto you, the Son can do nothing of himself, but what he seeth the Father do: for what things soever he doeth, these also doeth the Son likewise."....

In verse 23, Jesus speaks about His Father is in him: "...He that honoureth not the Son honoureth not the Father which hath sent him." Jesus said that all of His power comes from His Father: (24)"....Then came the Jews round about Him, and said unto Him, how long dost thou make us to doubt? If thou be the Christ, tell us plainly. Jesus answered them: "I told you, and ye believed not: the works that I do in my Father's name, they bear witness of me. But ye believe not, because ye not are not of my sheep, as I said unto you...."(29)"My Father, which gave them me, is greater than all; and no man is able to pluck them out of my Father's hand. I and my Father are one." (32)"....Many good works have I shewed you from My Father; for which of those works do ye stone me?"(John 10:24-32); continuing in verse 33, "The Jews answered Him, saying, for a good work we stone thee not; but for blasphemy; and because that thou, being a man, makest thyself God,(34) Jesus answered them: ....."(37)"If I do not the works of my Father, believe me not." (38)"But if I do, though ye believe not me, believe the works: that ye may know, and believe, that the FATHER IS IN ME, AND I IN HIM." (39)"Therefore they sought again to take him: but He escaped out of their hand...into Jordan..."(John 10). "I can of mine own self do nothing: as I hear, I judge: and my judgment is just; because I seek not mine own will, but the will of the Father which hath sent me"(John 5:30).

Another teaching from Jesus of him only doing the will and power through his Father to a man named Philip who asked: "Lord, shew us the Father, and it sufficeth us. (9) Jesus saith unto him: "'Have I been so long time with you, and yet hast thou not known me, Philip? He that hath seen me hath seen the Father; and how sayest thou then, Shew us the Father? (10).....Believest thou not that I am in the Father, and the Father in me? The words that I speak unto you I speak not of myself: but the Father that dwelleth in me, he doeth the works"'(John 14:9-10);as mentioned, God is too powerful to see.

Another powerful evidence that Jesus, refuse to just acknowledge himself as being the influence of miracles and power is what He said here: "He that believeth on me, believeth not on me, but on HIM that sent me. And he that seeth me seeth Him that sent me. I am come a light into the world, that whosoever believeth on me should not abide in darkness. And if any man hear my words, and believe not, I judge him not: for I came not to judge the world, but to save the world. He that rejected me, and receiveth not my words, hath one that judgeth him: the word that

I have spoken, the same shall judge him in the last day. For I have not spoken of myself; but the Father which sent me, He gave me a commandment is life everlasting: whatsoever I speak therefore, even as the Father said unto me, so I speak"(John 12:44-50.)

This is other evidence of what was discussed in chapter 1 that we, even Jesus CAN NOT do ANYTHING without the Head Father!! This is why the Jews couldn't understand after Jesus was hung on the cross, that He couldn't do anything about it; and Jesus asked His Father, "why have you forsaken me?" Because God, His Father, willingly removed all the powers given to Jesus so that he may be sacrificed. However, while on Earth, Jesus had all power through the will of His Father given to him. Jesus said that, "My Father loves me, because I lay down my life, that I might take it again. No man taketh it from me, but I lay it down of myself. I have power to lay it down, and I have power to take it again. This commandment have I received from my Father"(John 10:17-18).

Many people refuse to believe the powers and talents that God had given to Jesus. However, in John 5:46, Jesus explained to the Jews that: "If ye believed in Moses, you should believe me as well: for Moses wrote of me." In addition, Moses was with Jesus during His transfiguration: "...And behold, there appeared unto them Moses and Elias talking with Him" (Matthew 17:3). But what people fail to understand, is that the purpose of talents and powers is to be a blessing to another, and these talents were given by certain people to enable the blessing. You and I are that certain individual that can use these talents to serve our purposes. Until a talent is given, a person may find it very difficult to believe that they can perform it. God doesn't give everyone a talent that they may not need. This is where being chosen to exercise the talent comes in.

Though we were created equal and above the animals, we all have different spirit levels and powers within us. As mentioned in chapter 1, there are certain spirits that are more powerful than others, and even when they incarnate, that certain power remains within the individual to enable its use on Earth as in the case with Jesus, and other powerful incarnates. But because of Satan's wrath, these powerful incarnates still have to experience physical and emotional pain, and still was born into sin; which was the reason of Jesus' baptismal. Because of the power that remained in certain incarnates, this will cause them to overcome Satan's influence on Earth. But not all spirits have the ability to use certain powers or talents, because their spirits are not on a certain level of power and ability.

God created higher and lower spirits that incarnated into man. Here are a few verses that shows evidence of certain spiritual levels in mortals and immortals: (16)...."And many of the children of Israel shall he turn to the Lord their God. (17)And he shall go before him in the spirit and power of Elias, to turn their hearts of the fathers to the children....(18) And Zacharias said unto the angel, whereby shall I know this? For I am an old man, and my wife well stricken in years. (19) And the angel answering said unto him, "I am Gabriel, that stand in the presence of God; and am sent to speak unto thee, and to shew thee these glad tidings".(20) And behold, thou shalt be dumb, and not able to speak, until the day that these things shall be performed, because thou believest not my words, which shall be full filled in their season'"(Luke 1:16-20).

There was a time not long after Jesus' death, that Peter, one of His disciples performed miracles also, one of them were: (36)"Now there was at Joppa a certain disciple named Tabitha, which by interpretation is called Dorcas: this woman was full of good works...(37) And it came to pass...that she was sick, and died...... (40)Then Peter put them all forth, and kneeled down, and prayed; and turning him to the body said, Tabitha, arise. And she opened her eyes: and when she saw Peter, she sat up"(Acts 9:36-40)...."And when he had called unto him his twelve disciples, He (Jesus) gave them power against unclean spirits, to cast them out, and to heal all manner of sickness and all manner of disease"(Matthew 10). Jesus also declared to us that He gave us power: "Behold, I give you power to tread on serpents and scorpions and over all the power of the enemy; and nothing shall by any means hurt you"...(Luke 10:19).....'Ye have not chosen me, but I have chosen you, and ordained you, that ye should go and bring forth fruit, and that your fruit should remain: that whatsoever ye shall ask of the Father in my name, he may give it to you"(John 15:15-16).... (9)"I pray for them: I pray not for the world, but for them which thou hast given me; for they are thine. (10) And all mine are thine, and thine are mine; and I am glorified in them....(14) I have given them thy word; and the world hath hated them, because they are not of the world, even as I not of the world".....(18) "As thou hast sent me into the world, even so have I also sent them into the world" ....(21) That they all may be one; as thou, Father, art in me, and I in thee, that they also may be one in us..." (John 17:9-21).

God not only had His influence and power to His son Jesus, but also to other mortal men like in the cases of Moses and Elisha. When Moses parted the Red Sea, that was an influence by the power of God: "'And the Lord said unto Moses, "stretch out thine hand over the land of Egypt for the locusts, that they may come up upon the land of Egypt, and eat every herb of the land, even all that the hail hath left." (13) And Moses stretched forth his rod over the land of Egypt, and the Lord brought an east wind upon the land all that day.....the east wind brought the locusts"(Exodus 10:12-13).....(15)'"And the Lord said unto Moses, "wherefore criest thou unto me? Speak unto the children of Israel, that they go forward: (16) But lift thou up thy rod, and stretch out thine hand over the sea, and divide it: and the children of Israel shall go on dry ground through the midst of the sea....."'(21) "And Moses stretched out his hand over the sea; and the Lord caused the sea to go back by a strong east wind all that night, and made the sea dry land, and the waters were divided....(22) And the children of Israel went into the midst of the sea upon the dry ground: and the waters were a wall unto them on their right hand, and on their left. (23) And the Egyptians pursued,....(25) And took off their chariot wheels, that they drave them heavily..... (27) And Moses stretched forth his hand over the sea, and the sea returned to his strength when the morning appeared....and the Lord overthrew the Egyptians in the midst of the sea....(28) And the waters returned, and covered the chariots....and all the host of Pharaoh..."(Exodus 14:15-28). Another powerful spiritual influence that had occurred through God was in the days of King Ahaziah that was in Elisha: "(20)...And Elisha died, and they buried him. And the bands of the Moabites invaded the land at the coming in of the year. (21) And it came to pass, as they were burying a man, that, behold, they pled a band of men; and they cast the man into the sepulchre of Elisha: and when the man was let down, and touched the bones of Elisha, he revived, and stood up on his feet"(2 Kings 13:20-21).

These are just some of the powers that certain people of God had, who were chosen in the New as well as the Old Testaments in addition to Jesus. Some people may say, "I never performed miracles, or possessed those types of powers, and never seen anyone else in my lifetime that had done so either; that's why I don't believe in supernatural powers or in God, for that matter!" Maybe if you use a search engine and type miracles, or its adjectives like in the case of this source from the web: "After battling heart disease and lupus,.... for a heart transplant is miraculously healed" (www.cbn.com/media/index.aspx?s=/vod/GW91). This and other sources like this one can be used as evidence that God still performs miracles, even today! Also, a program was watched on the Nat Geo channel about a man and a bear that attacked him: miraculously after the man yelled "oh God, I don't want to die today", the bear mysteriously walked away! As Jesus explained, that was mentioned, we are chosen by Him, not us choosing Him.

And since all men do not have the same spirits, they will not have the same powers and abilities either.

This is why certain people can only handle or do certain things, whether bad or good. Others may have asked you questions, or vice versa like: 'how did you do that?' Or, "how were you able to do this?" Many would not respond by saying, 'because it is God who gave me the spirit to perform this"; but instead, they would say, "I don't know, I just have it in me", without realizing that it is their spirit that caused their ability to do certain things. There are spirits that can tolerate one extreme to the other, such as: lower spirits that incarnate as a transient who begs for food; or one who incarnates as a person of palsy, that otherwise, another spirit formed of a higher level would not be able to tolerate. This is a clue of why Jesus stated that the poor will be with you always: "For ye have the poor always with you; but me ye have not always"(Matthew 26:11);

He was referring to Himself of not being on Earth forever, but during our lifetime and beyond, the poor will always be present, and Jesus knew that the poor had a certain spirit. Because these are spirits of lower levels that incarnated to be this way for a purpose of allowing man to show love and kindness. On the other hand, there are spirits of higher levels that incarnate as kings, judges, and those of great financial status, and the like. These spirit types may not tolerate being incarnated as lower spirit levels; just as lower spirit types may not tolerate the feeling of over-abundance. Many privileged people would rather die than to be in a position of a lower person, because they can't mentally handle the pressures of being poor. Likewise, some people of lowered-level spirits are not able to handle the greater responsibilities of success.

God has the power to give wealth, to make poor, or rich: "And thou say in thine heart, My power and the might of mine hand hath gotten me this wealth. But thou shalt remember the Lord thy God: for it is He that giveth thee power to get wealth, that He may establish his covenant which He swore unto thy fathers, as it is this day"(Deuteronomy 8:17-18); …. "(7)The Lord maketh poor, and maketh rich: He bringeth low, and lifteth up.(8)He raiseth up the poor out of the dust,and lifteth up the beggar from the dunghill, to set them among princes, and make them inherit the throne of glory: for the pillars of the earth are the Lord's, and He hath set the world upon them"(1Samuel 2:7-8). So, this proves that we all are not equal in spirit, and no matter what you do or pray for, you will only receive of what was meant for you, and shall NOT refuse to believe what had happened to others, had not happened to you. This is why from one of the Ten Commandments states that you shall not covet thy neighbor's wife, because God gave the wife to him, and not to you. Anything that wasn't given to you should not be wanted or coveted from others' possessions, because it was not meant for you to have it to begin with. Likewise, if someone wants something that you have, they shall not want or covet of what's yours. No matter how little or how much you have, there is someone who may always want what you have, and no one is immune as being a victim of jealously or envy. Not getting what you want is not an easy feeling to handle if it's not meant for it to be in your life. This is the most controversial area where people have doubt, unbelief and skepticism about God and how He works. Even Jesus didn't have His prayer answered while in Gethsemane in Matthew 26:36 to avoid being crucified, because it was meant to happen.

As mentioned in chapter 1, the Prophet Jeremiah was told by God that he was ordained to be a prophet, just as He ordained many others who wrote the bible that should be respected and taken seriously. If one could believe what their palm reader tells them, which many will ask you whether you believe in God or not, should also believe the prophets that wrote the bible. As explained of what Jesus had said: "I have chosen you, not you chosen Me, and ordained you"(John 15:16). Jesus performed many miracles, because, as mentioned, for those who believe and were chosen by Jesus, was able to do the miracles through his Father. But many may wonder why miracles do not happen in their lives, or why they not able to perform them. It's because of their unbelief or the lack of being chosen. In Matthew 13:58, Jesus was in a place where people didn't believe the miracles He could perform, so because of their unbelief, He could not perform any: "And he did not many mighty works there because of their unbelief". The miracles and the teachings that Jesus performed is what put Him on the cross, after being found guilty of treason. However, before being accused of this crime and performing the miracles from his Father, Jesus had spoken with His disciples, and stated to all of them that one of them was going to betray Him. After another disciple, named Peter, heard this and said to Jesus that he would stay by Him, even until death. But Jesus told Peter that before the cock crows, three times you will deny me; Peter and the other disciples insisted that they never would.

Sadly, one evening from a place called Gethsemane, Jesus brought Peter and two others to talk with Him, as if He was afraid of what is about to happen to Him, while He instructed the other disciples to remain in their place while He goes to pray. First, Jesus spoke with the three men that came with Him saying: "My soul is exceeding sorrowful, even unto death: tarry ye here, and watch with me." Secondly, Jesus prayed to His Father so hard, that he sweated heavily as if large drops of blood came from him: to allow his Father's sacrifice to be passed over him; but Jesus said in his prayer: "Not my will, but let thine will be done." While Jesus was reciting this prayer, the three that came with Him had fallen asleep, and Jesus awaken them stating, "why you couldn't watch me for one hour?" Jesus left them and prayed again; then again returned to the sleeping disciples, and allowed them to sleep and went to pray the third time. As Jesus was returning, and speaking to them, Judas came with a great multitude of people with swords and staves from the chief priests and elders. Judas, one of the twelve disciples, betrayed Jesus with a kiss and the chiefs took and arrested Him; while some disciples fought against the chiefs, and one of them cut off one of their ears, Jesus miraculously replaced it. The remaining disciples forsook Him, and fled. Jesus was taken to Caiaphas the high priest while Peter followed Jesus afar off into the place where Jesus was under trial. After Peter arrived there, someone recognized him and stated that he was one of the disciples, which Peter denied three times before the cock crowed, as Jesus had foretold Peter. After Peter realized what he had done, he and Jesus starred at each other; Peter ran off and cried violently(Matthew 26:36-75).

After this, is when the abuse of Jesus had begun. He was severely beaten by a whip to the point that He was nearly swimming in His own blood and survived! There is supporting evidence that Jesus was foretold throughout the Old Testament, and He did indeed was chastised with many stripes; one of the foretold verses, including the one in the New Testament: "Surely He hath borne our griefs, and carried our sorrows: yet we did esteem Him stricken, smitten of God, and afflicted. But He was wounded for our transgressions, He was bruised for our iniquities: the chastisement of our peace was upon him; and with His stripes we are healed"(Isaiah 53:4-5);…"Who His own self bare our sins in His own body on the tree, that we, being dead to sins, should live unto righteousness: by His stripes ye were healed"(1 Peter 2:24). Both of these verses were referring to Jesus. In addition His abuse was including being slapped; pushed and kicked around; was spat on; was sent to prison bound in chains; was betrayed and denied by two of His disciples; He walked and carried the cross, and was abused while doing so, after being found guilty of treason, sentenced to crucifixion and went through severe pain while on the cross for over nine hours, dying a slow agonizing death! Asking His Father, "why have You forsaken me?" After this, Jesus cried with a loud voice, died and gave up the ghost, was resurrected after three days in His tomb, and eventually ascended back to Heaven with His Father.

But why does it seems that many had speculated that Jesus died at around age thirty? It was at this age is when He was baptized, and the Holy Ghost appeared to Him descending toward Him as a dove, that is stated in Luke 3:22-23. Many other events occurred between that time up until His crucifixion from arriving in Jerusalem on a donkey; raised Lazareth from the dead; was led by the Spirit into the wilderness for 40 days being tempted by Satan; and many other events that started after Luke 3:23 up to the arrest in Luke 22. In addition, there are two other speculations that it was not so, that Jesus died at thirty: "...Thou art not yet fifty years old, and hast thou seen Abraham?"..."Verily, verily, I say unto you, before Abraham was, I am"(John 8:57-58). So, if He died at 30, why would the Jews speculate to Jesus 20 years ahead of this age that he wasn't fifty years old yet? Apparently, Jesus was either right at 30 years or older, but younger than 50. From another verse, Jesus compared a temple to His body: "".... Destroy this temple, and in three days I will raise it up. Then said the Jews: "Forty and six years was this temple in building, and wilt thou rear it up in three days?" But He spake of the temple of His body""(John 2:19-21).

If Jesus had died on the cross at 30, the 46 years that it took to build the temple that the Jews were referring to would have seemed to conflict the Jews' comparison of 46 years of building the temple. In addition to this possible evidence, is when Jesus was baptized by John the Baptist: "...(32)And John bare record, saying, I saw the Spirit descending from heaven like a dove, and it abode upon Him. (33)And I knew not: but He that sent me to baptize with water, the same said unto me, upon whom thou shalt see the Spirit descending, and remaining on Him, the same is He which baptizeth with the Holy Ghost. (34)And I saw, and bare record that this is the Son of God"...(John 1:32-34). This verse is a repeat of the one in Luke 3:22 that stated Jesus was about 30 years old, and also the verse that was BEFORE the verse in John 2. Jesus was not meant to live a very long time on Earth, because as God wanted sacrifices for animals to be without blemishes, spots, young, and in good health, His Son had to be the same way along with having the strength to carry the cross for His crucifixion and sacrifice.

All of this happened, because of one man betrayed Him. But did this man, Judas, betrayed Jesus in vain? Did Judas knew exactly what he was doing when he betrayed Jesus? What or who possessed him to become the betrayer? A clue to these questions to whether Judas innocently betrayed or betrayed Jesus in vain is very difficult to analyze: "Then Judas, which had betrayed Him, when he saw that He was condemned, repented himself, and BROUGHT again the thirty pieces of silver to the chief priests and elders, saying, I have sinned in that I have betrayed innocent blood. And they said, what is that to us? See thou to that. And he cast down the pieces of silver in the temple, and departed, and hanged himself"(Matthew 27:3-5). But from another verse, it seems that he knew what he was doing: "'Then one of the twelve, called Judas Iscariot, went unto the chief priests, and said unto them, "what will ye give me, and I will deliver Him unto you?" And they covenanted with him for thirty pieces of silver'"(Matthew 26:14-16).

After all the discussion of Jesus from how He was born and died, what is your feeling about this? How did it affect you? Do you believe, or what is your opinion about Jesus? Do you still have doubt about Him? Why, or why not? Do you believe the miracles He performed? Do you believe that He walked the Earth and is the Son of the Most High God? Why, or why not? Think for a moment of how can you answer these questions about Jesus and your opinion on Him, and read the bible about believing and confessing with your mouth that He is the Son of God, and you believe that He came and died for your sins, and if you do, according to the bible, you will be saved. This means, that your sins will be forgiven as a born-again Christian, and you will be able to go to Heaven and remain there forever. Now you are saying, "so what? I still don't believe in any of this, because I don't see people performing miracles anymore; and need to know before I do believe: why miracles aren't being performed like the stories in the bible anymore?" "Why should I even believe in God or other supernatural beings?" Or believe that Jesus is the Messiah? In one verse He stated to a woman whom He asked for a drink while walking that He is the Messiah: "'The woman said unto Him, "I know that Messias cometh, which is called Christ: when he is come, he will tell us all things". Jesus said unto her, "I that speak unto thee am he"'(John 4:25-26). Think for a for a moment, if you were living during the time Jesus walked on Earth, would you still believe? This seemed to be one chance of a lifetime to see Him, compared to others who never have. But, even some people that lived during this time, still didn't believe. Jesus had done miracles and commonly things like preaching and eating right in front of them and they still thought that it was a joke. There are many who not only believe in Jesus, but not in God also. As mentioned in chapter one, God created everything that is seen and unseen, and what was mentioned earlier in this chapter is that if it's not meant for you, it will not happen.

However, if you include the billions upon billions of cells; the wind; the spirits that are in Heaven and the ones that dwell within us; the evaporated water that is a gas; the vitamins and minerals that runs through our blood that keep our bodies functioning and healthy; the plants that do their jobs of exchanging CO_2 and O_2; even the events of exchanging of gases while we breathe; radioactive waves that are too powerful to see, and so much, much, more are just pieces of the unseen operations of life and other phenomena that is incredible, and yet we believe many things like these that either can't be seen or are too powerful to see! In John 1:18, and as mentioned in other verses from earlier chapters, that: "No man hath seen God at any time....(John 1). Jesus wants us all to believe in His Father and in Him, because we are a part of Him that was created in His Father's image and likeness. Again, this book is not intended to persuade a belief in Him. However, it is intended for those whom are having a difficult time of exercising this belief to ask others who and why they do, and ask why should you believe and explain the details of why you shouldn't believe in Jesus or God, and how His creations came about.

But explain to the many how did nature and other things became the miracle, or created itself. How did nature existed on its own? If nature was this powerful, the things in it, including us wouldn't be able to withstand itself. It takes an intellect being or other phenomenon to make everything exist and work. In order to be a creator, the being must be able to withstand the elements that make creation possible, like: radiation, extreme temperatures to create: rocks, icebergs, volcanoes, the sun, etc. Even made-made chemicals and elements have to be handled with care, and the developer must be protected while handling the chemicals being made, these chemicals didn't make themselves. What created the trillions of stars, planets, galaxies, black holes, gases, and many other unexplainable objects in space? What part of nature has this great power to create the universe, which is possibly endless? Show or explain to us readers a possible creator of all that's around us, and maybe we'll have something to talk about. "Jesus had done so much, that even the world would not contain all that would be written, A-men"(John 21:25). Now that you have read about Jesus and His works and maybe interested in knowing Him better, by practicing and following His teachings. Moreover, you want to know what He looks like, what is His race, and other physical characteristics after He descended as a mortal man. Visit this web source and see what you think: http://www.popularmechanics. com/science/health/forensics/1282186.

There are biblical sources that describes Jesus' hair as being wooly, and as white as wool with a dark brass-like skin tone in Daniel 7:9 and Revelation 1:14-15. Also, visit: http://www. religioustolerance.org/chr_jcfa.htm . If you read additional verses in the bible, there is proof that God's image and race could be of

Judean descent, and Jesus is the exact image and replica of God: "For it is evident that our Lord sprang out of Juda; of which tribe Moses spake nothing concerning priesthood" (Hebrews 7:14); another verse that speaks of God's heritage: "I will also gather all nations, and will bring them down into the valley of Jehoshaphat, and will plead with them there for my people and for my heritage Israel, whom they have scattered among the nations, and parted my land"(Joel 3:2). Israel is the name that God gave to Jacob in Gen. 32:28, and represented the tribe of Judah, which was one of Jacob's 12 sons. To get a better understanding of Israel and the truth about the original Jews, please visit: http://www.stewartsynopsis. com/Isreal.htm . As mentioned in chapter 3, Jesus' descent goes way back to Abraham to David. This is why God claims Himself as the "God of Abraham, Isaac, and Jacob", because He and the following 3 are descents of the Judean Tribe.

We all were created in God's image and likeness. Being in likeness doesn't always mean to resemble or look like someone, but to be in likeness of copying characteristics, instincts, and intellect. God wants us to be fruitful and multiply. This is why He had to do the same before we were created, to bring forth His son Jesus, and created the heavens for His, Jesus', and other dwellers' home. Then He created mortality for sacrifice of blood, which He sent His son Jesus to do for us to prove His love towards us. We are the living, mortal image of God, and He gave us freewill and knowledge to make choices of good and evil; one of many characteristics of a god.

Chapter 4

OUR PURPOSES: CHARACTERISTICS, REINCARNATION, AND EMOTIONS

Now that you have read how we were created and the purpose of evil, you now want to know why we were created and what is our purpose. Chapters 2 and 3 discussed how evil was born and how we were redeemed from the effects of the evil that God imposed upon mankind through Satan. Chapter 2 explained the purpose of evil, which was to test man's faith and obedience in God. Many wonder why do we have to endure evil in order to serve a purpose. Why evil has to accompany everything we do? Others may also ask, why did we have to come to Earth to serve a purpose, and just serve the purpose in Heaven forever instead? If we are chosen for a specific purpose, why do some serve a purpose through evil, like in the case of Judas, whom Jesus had chosen?

Many are perplexed to why it seems in order for something good to happen, evil has to accompany the event. In order for good things to surface, we MUST endure or even welcome the evil event that occurred. This is part of successfully serving our purpose, by using evil as a teaching and guiding tool. Using this tool will affect your emotions and integrity along with your mental and physical attributions. The collaboration of using our eternal spirit, mind, and physical powers usually comes from an event that caused all three characteristics to come into one purpose of incarnation. But have you considered the reason for reincarnation? Or why you should or should not believe in it? Before reincarnation is discussed further, emotions and the characteristics of each type, reason for evil in accompanying our purpose, will be explained first.

In order to understand why we must go through evil events just to serve a purpose, the emotions and characteristics in dealing with the aspects of it will be analyzed by detail. Serving our purpose for God can be very frustrating at times. All frustrations come from the evil influences that accompany it.

Frustrations can lead to depression, anxiety, confusion, and negativity. As mentioned in chapter 3, each spirit that a man possesses has various levels of tolerance and power. God will not allow a spirit to incarnate into a location or situation that it may not be able to handle for carnal survival. There are a few biblical verses that support God's way of not allowing situations or events to overtake us: "There hath no temptation taken you but such as is common to man; but God is faithful, who will not suffer you to be tempted above that ye are able: but will with the temptation also make way to escape, that ye may be able to bear it"(1Cor. 10:13); ...."When thou passest through the waters, I will be with thee: and through the rivers, they shall not overflow thee: when thou walkest through the fire, thou shalt not be burned; neither shall the flame kindle upon thee"(Isaiah 43:2); ..."God is our refuge and strength, a very present help in trouble...The Lord of hosts is with us; the God of Jacob is our refuge"(Psalms 46); ..."Surely He shall deliver thee from the snare of the fowler, and from the noisome pestilence" (Psalms 91:3).

Without God placing a spirit to where it should be, can cause the body that it dwells in to serve an incomplete purpose resulting from death. A spirit that leaves a dead or a fatally traumatized body doesn't always come from an accidental event. A person's emotions and attitude can affect the body greatly. These bad emotions can lead to mental and physical illnesses that could possibly shorten a life. The two major mental disturbances that can lead to death are depression and anxiety. Minor ones like confusion and negativity can only distract a person to focus on the right direction. But you're thinking if God correctly combine the right spirit with the right body, why are people still getting depressed, or don't have faith in themselves? The possible answers to this question can be numerous. The first answer could be that since evil involves everything from: negativity, doubt, lack of faith, fear, lack of interest, confusion, or even to complacency can result from lack of confidence or interest in finding a purpose.

The second possible answer to this question is that people have a tendency to be jealous or want something that the other has. This attitude can lead into another evil influence such as hate, depression, or envy. People who exercise this evil habit don't realize, all they're doing is creating additional problems in their lives. Instead of accepting who they are by needing to know that everyone is not created spiritually equal, and there are others whom could be envy or jealous of them as well. No matter how much or less a person has, there will always be another that will envy the other, whether physical, mental, or material possessions are involved.

In the case of Job, whom was mentioned in chapter 2, was a person who seemed to have not deserved what God had done to him through Satan. Job was one of the richest men in the east, and was a faithful man to God. For some reason, Job was punished over something he didn't do, and yet God gave and took everything from him, including his children! This seems to indicate that this was a test of limitation, which can happen to anyone. Most souls that incarnated would not be able to handle this type of test of this magnitude. God puts a stress limit upon each of us. But still, many would find it confusing of why a man like Job, who was perfect in God's sight would be cursed so harshly as if he was nearly sacrificed like Jesus? One thing Job said from a verse: "This is one thing, therefore I said it, He destroyeth the perfect and the wicked"(Job 9:22). Though God said that Job was perfect and upright, it seemed that his sons was not so, according to a verse in the Book of Job: "….Job sent and sanctified them, and rose up early in the morning, and offered burnt offerings according to the number of them all: for Job said, it may be that my sons have sinned, and cursed God in their hearts…."(Job 1:5). Now, why would Job suspect that his sons may have sinned and cursed God in their hearts unless he felt or knew that they had done so beforehand? Unless there is a witness, one person wouldn't suspect another of an act if it's unusual for that person to commit it. If he knew that his sons were perfect like him, it seems that job wouldn't think a such accusation of his sons' sins, which makes it easier to understand why God may have taken all of Job's children.

But why Job himself was cursed, if he was perfect and upright? Could this test of limitation could have now turned into a test of faith? Now that Job's sons are gone, this could have been a test of Job's love for God, to not only love Him when things are going well; just as Jesus loved his Father even when things weren't going so well! Likewise what was mentioned in chapter 2, is that God knew that He created Satan for a purpose. That purpose was to test our limitation and endurance of the pestilence and pain. God has freewill like man, and could have spared Satan away from us. However, since that didn't happen, this is why He want us to love Him even after He caused Satan to disrupt our lives, and likewise, He loves us, though we sin through our freewill. Maybe that's why so many people still sin, because they know that Satan causes them to sin, but God is in control and should be able to do something about Satan, and feel as if God don't care what Satan do to them; leaving them here on Earth to tackle with him without fault of their own. Many of us use negative guides like depression, doubt, drugs, or giving up as ways to deal with negative forces in life. Many of us think that God is not comfortable or pleased when man is at his happiest with everything that is given to him.

This is why depression and anxiety can swing both ways, while a person is doing great or not so great. Many of us, like Job had either prepared for the worst or just doing the right thing like: offering sacrifices for his sons' sins, going to church, offering praises to God, and bad things still happened anyway that lead into depression, anxiety, and confusion, leaving us to figure: "why bother?"

Depression is when, after something that had happened makes a person become sad and withdraw. They felt that no matter what they did, bad or good, something was either taken away from them or it never came to offer relief in their life. Many who go through this period feel that they have no power to rise against this setback. However, many fail to realize how dangerous depression can be if allowed to linger too long. From a source on depression, explains the effects that can be fatal: heart disease could arise that can cause inflammation of the blood vessels, causing blood clots that lead to a heart attack. Pain from having depression usually starts with headaches and back pain that didn't come from physical strain. The cause of the pain is related to a chemical imbalance in the brain, which is controlled by the pituitary gland. This gland controls how all hormones are released throughout the body. When depression sets in, many hormones in the brain and muscles are affected, which causes the pain. Sleep can be affected from problems of depression.

Insufficient amounts of sleep can result from chronic diseases like diabetes, obesity, high blood pressure, and alcohol abuse that can shorten the lifespan. Problems with sleep mostly come from depression. The signs of sleeping problems from depression are: difficulty of falling asleep; awakening frequently; and an inability to sleep. Some people may over-sleep while suffering from depression. Sexual dysfunction can result from many areas, but often, it comes from depression that result from lack of interest, or obtaining an erection. The immune system is affected by depression from inflammation of the entire body from a chemical known as cytokines, which cause autoimmune disorders such as Crohn's disease, arthritis, and psoriasis, including Alzheimer's disease, frequent infections, and cancer. Poor appetite can result from depression that can cause a person to over or under eat: from Kathleen Blanchard. Depression basically affects the whole body that could lead to suicidal thoughts or death.

After a person had prayed or spoke to others about their problems, anxiety can set in after desperation of needed relief if neither prayer nor other resources solved the problem, creating a stressful event or situation. Anxiety is different from depression by which, a person becomes either worried or frightened, verses to becoming sad. This disorder can affect the body like depression, and is the most common human reaction to stress. The symptoms are: depersonalization (feeling of separation from body); strong, irregular heartbeats; difficulty breathing or swallowing; feelings of collapse, or muscle weakness or trembling; and sweaty palms. The effects of anxiety are: feelings of irritability, depression, hostility, guilt, self-criticism, negative thoughts, excessive dependency on others; inability of handling stressful situations like exams and interviews; phobias, irrational worries; problems with coping with everyday problems, and functioning efficiently. If you think that you may have anxiety, find ways to seek treatment. Anxiety can be controlled by hypnosis. To learn more on using this technique visit: www.reduce-your-anxiety.com/index.html; there, you will see a menu to the right that has clickable articles on each subject on anxiety.

Both depression and anxiety can lead to drug and alcohol abuse. People who use drugs and alcohol to cope, think that they are doing their mind and body good by an illusion of escaping from reality. It may feel good temporarily, but the fix is only short-lived. Though many may know this, why people still do it? If they recover or sober up, the problems are still with them. The time and money spent on using alcohol or drugs could have been used on other ways on solving many issues that a person may have. As long as this person continues to abuse alcohol or drugs, the problems can remain with them longer than anticipated, instead of using other ways of solving them by shortening the time. Believe it or not, people think it's a mature, ego way of coping while abusing drugs or alcohol, not realizing that all it is, is an addiction, which is a sign of weakness. Drug addicts are considered weak, because the drug is controlling them, and them not controlling it. The strong and champions do not let or want anything to control them! They would rather fight or have the determination to not allow any substance to overtake them.

In order for you to be the same way, first you must think of yourself as strong, and that you can do this. "For as he thinketh in his heart, so is he...."(Proverbs 23:7). Whatever you think of yourself, that's who you are. If you think you're weak, that is who you are, and by identifying yourself in such a negative way you will always be an addict or considered weak. To think of yourself as being a champion, think of the good qualities about you as well as others, and think that nobody is perfect and there are good and bad qualities in everyone and in everything. Even though others may not be an addict like you, they also may have other habits that are not supportive in solving their problems like physical or genetic issues, and yet remain strong. Under these conditions, when certain problems may not be solved think of the good things that you are able to solve. God didn't create everybody to solve every problem, we are not omnipotent like Him, and should not compare Him or others in judgment to yourself. Only judge yourself favorably, without thinking only on the negatives you have. Even champions have weaknesses, but they know how to focus only on their strengths without using them against themselves and others. As long as you focus on this attitude, you can come a long way by alleviating the burden of anxiety and depression.

To further relieve the burden of both anxiety and depression, thinking and speaking positive of yourself can help tremendously. Even if the outcome doesn't look promising, focusing on the positive strengthens self-esteem. Once self-esteem strengthens, will-power can motivate you to move forward in a positive direction. The feelings of negativity will soon turn into a positive mode of motivation. Negativity can destroy self-esteem and even the feeling of self-worthiness. If a person uses negativity throughout life, it can override all other aspects of positives that leads into depression, low self-esteem, anxiety, and complacency. Negativity rules over all of these characters.

In order to defeat a negative attitude, you must be able to understand God's purpose. Most find this area in life difficult to accomplish. Some have died, and still never understood why they were here. Many people may wonder, why God makes it so difficult for one to find their purpose instead of just guiding a person to the right direction, to prevent many other directions that were a waste of time? Why do we have to make so many mistakes to find a purpose? Serving a purpose is not only doing something for God, but also a teaching tool to enable oneself to increase wisdom or strength for preparation for a better purpose. Every purpose requires baby steps. Though God may have a purpose for you to be a doctor, you have to go through childhood and college for this great purpose to take place. Yes, there will be mistakes along the way, but mistakes enable a person to learn other options other than what's in a book.

Mistakes build many characteristics in a person like: determination, ambition, hope, integrity, and maturity. Mistakes like forgetting or ignorance either by reason or coincidence should be taken as a reward instead of a punishment. Say if you forgot something that was costly that had to be replaced, but you replaced it with something better or more rewarding than the original item.

Another, so-called bad experience could be while you're driving, and all of a sudden a flat tire, you are in despair and was able to drive to a shop that enabled you to meet the husband of your dreams! Finding one's purpose can be an extremely difficult task, especially if it wasn't meant for you to begin with. Everyone was created for a specific purpose that had the right spirit to master the task. An inability to understand God's purpose for you can lead to depression, confusion, anxiety, frustration, and doubt with a feeling of unworthiness. In addition, this is one of the major issues why people are addicts, to keep their minds off of trying to figure things out. Some may think that they had found their purpose just to find out that all of the effort was a waste of time. The most important thing to avoid when trying to find your purpose is to not copy someone else's, because what their purpose is may not be yours. Certain spirits must serve a certain purpose. Likewise, the right battery must fit in order for something that needs it to work or serve a purpose of accommodating the item. A person should be happy serving a purpose, even just mopping floors for a living, because they have the correct spirit to get the job done for God, and should not envy another whose spirit may serve a higher purpose. Spirits that are at this high level may have had a rough start in life and rose to success. In contrast, there may be spirits whom had a great start that ended in tragedy, because it was either meant to be or by bad choices.

The same scenario happened while we were in Heaven, that we had it good and allowed Satan to overtaken us, which caused us to fall with him. This fall is called 'incarnation', which was God's way of giving us another chance, instead of sending us to eternal punishment called Hell. This place is the opposite of Heaven, everything God creates has its opposite. God loves us so much that He had to show Satan that he wasn't going win by taking all the hosts He created just to have them to fall at a point of no return. But in order to show God that we will not listen to Satan again, we could no longer live in Heaven without rectifying of what we did. This is where incarnation had to take place to correct our fallacies with showing greater love and appreciation for God. Many may ask though, if a spirit lives forever, how old is our spirit and how does God allows it to incarnate in a temporary, mortal body? Does God create new spirits every time somebody is born? Even if He did, where does the spirit goes after it leaves a body? Does the spirit goes back to Heaven or Hell, or does it just float 'out there' somewhere? What really happens when you die and what happens to the spirit? We know actually what happens to the body when it dies, but what about the eternal spirit? Even if it goes back to Heaven after a person dies without ever having a chance to pray, or ask for forgiveness, had incomplete tasks before leaving Earth; or never had a chance to see their kids grow up. It seems that some died without completing their purpose, and left it for someone else to finish it.

We all know that life as well as the entire universe is a cycle that repeats itself, because that's how God created it. Everything He created has the power to either reproduce or renew itself, absolutely everything!! So, if mortal things have this power, why wouldn't celestials, like spirits and other celestial beings have the same power? If something destroys a spider's web, it has the power to recreate it. The reason for re-creation is the condition of mortality from the remnants of evil. This caused everything, including spirits to recycle in order to re-correct any flaws from the evil forces that surrounds all environments. Without recreation nothing would exist. Though celestials are usually beings that don't die, they still have to either recycle or recreate themselves in order to meet the demands of a constant changing physical and celestial worlds; because celestials control the physical environment and mortal life. So, since mortal beings have the power to recreate and recycle, celestial beings must be able to do the same. Humans belong to two homes, one is temporary, and the other is eternal.

A spirit that comes from a celestial dwelling must incarnate into flesh and blood in order to be able to meet challenges against gravity, and a different atmosphere other than the heavens'. People who have died or had near-death experiences would not be able to allow mortal beings hear them speak, because different sound waves are in different atmospheres from theirs. This is why God created life that would match the atmosphere that it needs. People who had near-death experiences while trying to communicate with their friends and families couldn't hear them. As soon as the spirits of the people who had died returned to their bodies, they were able to hear the communication again from their love ones. When a person has a near-death experience, it is somewhat, a reincarnation, because their spirit left the body and returned.

Reincarnation is when a person dies, their spirit leaves the body and returns as a mortal individual. As mentioned earlier, everything that God created have the power to recreate or recycle of what was caused by destruction or wear and tear. Moreover, it was also mentioned that people had died without completing their purpose, and for some reason God only allowed tasks to not be completed by certain ones who left it for someone else to finish it. There are some reasons that may apply: certain people knew their purpose, but wasn't happy with it; some people are afraid of old age; some may have gotten into a severe accident that caused irreversible physical or mental trauma that limited their ability to complete their mission, and simply just lost their will to live; or some whom may have felt that they had completed their purpose, young or old, and just felt that they had done enough.

Here are a few biblical verses on possible evidence of reincarnation: "For, behold, I create new heavens and a new earth: and the former shall not be remembered, nor come into mind"(Isaiah 65:17); ....(9) "The thing that hath been, it is that which shall be..... and there is no new thing under the sun. (10) Is there anything whereof it may be said, see, this is new? It hath been already of old time, which was before us. (11) "There is no remembrance of former things; neither shall there be any remembrance of things that are to come with those that shall come after"(Ecclesiastes 1:9-11); "He hath made everything beautiful in His time: also He hath set the world in their heart, so that no man can find out the work that God maketh from the beginning to the end"(Ecclesiastes 3:11); (12)"And from the days of John the Baptist until now the kingdom of heaven suffered violence, and the violent take it by force. (13)For all the prophets and the law prophesied until John. (14)And if ye will receive it, this is this Elias, which was for to come"(Matthew 11:12-14);"And he shall go before him in the spirit and power of Elias, to turn the hearts of the fathers to the children..."(Luke 1:17); (10)... "And His disciples asked Him, saying, why then say the scribes that Elias must first come? (11)And Jesus answered and said unto them, Elias truly shall first come, and restore all things, (12)But I say unto you, that Elias is come already, and they knew him not...." (13) Then the disciples understood that He spake unto them of John the Baptist" (Matthew 17:10-13). But John 1:19-21, states: "And this is the record of John, when the Jews sent priests and Levites from Jerusalem to ask him, who art thou? (20) And he confessed, and denied not; but confessed, I am not the Christ. (21) And they asked him, what then? Art thou Elias? And he saith, I am not, art thou that prophet? And he answered, no". Now, why would Jesus claim that John the Baptist is Elias, but John denied himself as being Elias?

Reincarnation can be a confusing subject to believe or not to believe. If you read Hebrews 9:27, it will tell you that we live once, and later be judged. However, if you read again, Isaiah 65:17, God states that He creates new heavens and a new earth, and the former shall not be remembered, nor come into mind. What He is stating here is that we may live on this Earth once, but He creates or created another one. In Revelation 21, it seems that heaven and Earth were new: "And I saw a new heaven and a new earth: for the first heaven and the first earth were passed away, and there was no more sea." Isaiah 65:17 seems to be in the present tense, while Revelation 21 seems to be in the future tense of what John saw in his vision.

One indication that points out former or past times is where people can get confused: just because the bible speaks about former times, it doesn't always mean something that happened in our era. Just think for a moment, after reading Ecclesiastes 1:11 where it says, "there is no remembrance of former things...", the bible, of course would not obviously state a single lifetime or even several generations of events that occurred overtime, and expects a person to remember some or all of them. Wouldn't it be odd to you if someone asks or tells you something that happened a long time ago, if they weren't referring to your lifetime or generation? If someone asks you what did you remember seeing during World War II, you would ask them: "how would I remember?", this event was before my time! The prophets who wrote the bible knew what former things or times meant in God's perspective. They expected that God obviously knew that we wouldn't remember things before our lifetime, in this present era; we barely remember what happened during childhood, or even yesterday!

If our parents asked us do you remember what happened to you when you were little, this would be considered a long-term memory that happened while you were still in the same body. If you were asked did you remember what or how you did it the first time, this would be refreshing memory that someone may or may not want to remember, while still in the same body. Many people think after reading, "former things should not be remembered", they are only speculating past events that occurred during this era on the same earth. What many fail to understand, is that God is referring to eras of a constant recycling Earth, and this is where scientists get their estimate of the Earth's age of 4 billion years old. When God stated, "the former shall not be remembered", He meant the former Earth with its former times. He knew that He needed to address this, in order to differentiate His version of "former things" to the one of man's. When God creates a new

Earth, the old is completely burned and recycled. When you read Genesis 1:1-13, it took up to 3 days for God to create Earth. One day is a thousand years to God, just as former times is an era or ion to Him. So, when Moses wrote Genesis, what day was he referring to as far as time length? Was he referring to God's time or ours? It either could have taken God 3,000 days or three 24-days to create Earth. The timeline between creation of Earth and man is a large gap in time between either three to five 24-days, or 3 to 5 years in God's time.

The Earth abides forever according to Him, just as Jesus does, even though He came and died. Here are couple of verses that supports that the Earth does indeed last forever: "One generation passeth away, and another generation cometh: but the earth abideth forever" (Ecclesiastes 1:4); and,…"Who laid the foundations of the earth, that it should not be removed forever"(Psalms 104:5). Here's another verse that speaks about God's creation that seems to never be completely destroyed: (36) "His seed shall endure forever, and his throne as the sun before me. (37)It shall be established forever as the moon, and as a faithful witness in heaven.."(Psalms 89:36-37). Everything that God created, is never completely destroyed, it's either recycled or reborn. If He didn't destroy Satan, why would He destroy anything else? This is a verse that supports that Satan will not be completely destroyed: "And the devil that deceived them was cast into the lake of fire and brimstone, where the beast and the false prophet are, and shall be tormented day and night forever and ever"(Rev. 20:10). God has high priests who were given power of an endless life like Jesus, who continues as a high priest forever: (15) "And it is yet far more evident: for that after the similitude of Melchisedec there ariseth another priest. (16) Who is made, not after the law of a carnal commandment, but after the power of an endless life. (17) For He testifieth, thou art a priest forever after the order of Melchisedec…. (22)By so much was Jesus made a surety of a better testament. (23) And they truly were many priests, because they were not suffered to continue by reason of death:(24) But this man, because He continueth ever, hath an unchangeable priesthood" (Hebrews 7: 15-24)...(10)"By the which will we are sanctified through the offering of the body of Jesus Christ once for all. (11) And every priest standeth daily ministering and offering oftentimes the same sacrifices, which can never take away sins: (12)But this man, after he had offered one sacrifice for sins forever, sat down on the right hand of God..."(Hebrews 10:10-12).

If there were many priests whom had eternal lives, why so many were needed, as stated in verse 23? Unless one or two offered gifts and sacrifices of sins, and lives continuously. The amount of priests that this verse is referring to, may be of one priest; just as when God said of Him creating new heavens and a new Earth, though they are the same ones. Likewise, when we are born-again Christians we become a new creature as the bible states. Melchisedec or Melchezedec, king of Salem was a priest of the Most High God back in the days of Abraham. Melchisedec was named as an everlasting, high priest of God like Jesus: "Without father, without mother, without descent, having neither beginning of days, nor end of life; but made like unto the Son of God, abideth a priest continually"(Hebrews 7:3).

If we weren't reincarnated, why would God states that we shall not remember former times? As He said, "that the former shall not be remembered, nor come into mind". Our bodies wouldn't live that long of a time to remember God's work from the beginning to the present. Even if God showed us everything He done or will do from beginning to end, will we be able to remember every detail? More than likely, no. Otherwise, what does the verse in Isaiah really mean? If we were not reincarnated, was this verse referring to us while living in Heaven? Another point for us to think about is that, when God does renew the Earth where would the creatures and humans be? Or even when He creates new heavens and a new Earth, where would all the hosts and inhabitants of Earth be while the recycling process takes place? When God creates new heavens, the whole universe, which is considered as the heavens, there is no way that anything or anyone could survive the regenerating process of the entire universe. As mentioned in chapter 1, there are celestial beings that are not able to reside in certain parts of the universe, because of atmospheric reasons. No one knows how vast the universe is, and what all the atmospheric areas it contains, or what other beings that could be in them! So therefore, the area of the universe where heavenly hosts or other beings reside that God renews, have to be destroyed or destruction will occur among them anyway if they are placed in another area of the heavens while the regeneration takes place.

During regeneration of the entire universe, where the hosts and other beings reside that includes Earth, there is fire and powerful gases that are involved in the recycling process. While the Earth is being recycled, it's a total ball of fire that burns merely to nothing. Not only the Earth will be burned, but the heavens also will go through a recycling burning. Here's a verse that supports this: (10)"But the day of the Lord will come as a thief in the night; in the which the heavens shall pass away with a great noise, and the elements shall melt with fervent heat, the earth also and the works that are therein shall be burned up.(11) Seeing then that all these things shall be dissolved, what manner of persons ought ye to be in all holy conversation and godliness,(12)Looking for and hasting unto the coming of the day of the God, wherein the heavens being on fire shall be dissolved, and the elements shall melt with fervent heat?(13) Nevertheless we, according to his promise, look for new heavens and a new earth, wherein dwelling righteousness"(2Peter 3:10-13). The interesting fact about this parable, where will we be while all of this destruction and recycling for the new heavens and Earth is taking place? How long will it take for God to recycle the heavens?

As mentioned earlier, there is no possibility that we will be around to see all this takes place, and this is why reincarnation will more than likely take place to dwell on the new earth and heavens. Here is a verse that we and heaven will be rolled up and destroyed for the recycling process: (4)"And all the host of heaven shall be dissolved, and the heavens shall be rolled together as a scroll: and all their host shall fall down, as the leaf falleth off from the vine, and as a falling fig from the fig tree"....(8) For it is the day of the Lord's vengeance....." (Isaiah 34:4& 8). This is the Book of Isaiah's version to the end of the world. Here's another verse that speaks in the same similitude in the destruction of the heavens: (13)"And the stars of heaven fell unto the earth, even as a fig tree casteth her untimely figs, when she is shaken of a mighty wind. (14)And the heaven departed as a scroll when it is rolled together; and every mountain and island were moved out of their places"(Rev.6:13-14). Visit: http://www.unification.net/ dp73/dp73-1-3.html to get a better understanding on how God restores and different examples of "last days", or use keywords: where will we be while heaven and earth is being destroyed; no question mark needed. Another source that explains the "new earth and heaven" can be read at: http://www.sacred-texts.com/ chr/tbr/tbr094.htm .

Here, is another verse that may have even stronger support that God did indeed recreated a past Earth and heavens that was destroyed just like the present will be:(5)"For this they willingly are ignorant of, they by the word of God the heavens were of old, and the earth standing out of the water and in the water:(6) Whereby the world that then was, being overflowed with water, perished:(7) But the heavens and the earth, which are now, by the same word are kept in store, reserved unto fire against the day of judgment and perdition of ungodly men"(2 Peter 3:5-7).Please visit this source that will explain more in detail of the possible truth behind this: http://godskingdomfirst.org/GapTheory.htm. As mentioned earlier, God would not obviously write in a bible that would state certain times that we will understand unless He is referring to His timeline only: "were of old".

Also, another indication that it wasn't this earth that was officially destroyed by water, because God made a promise by a rainbow after the flood during Noah's time that He would not again let water flood to this magnitude ever again: "(12) And God said, this is the token of the covenant which I make between me and you and every living creature that is with you, for perpetual generations: (13) I do set my bow in the cloud, and it shall be for a token of a covenant between me and the Earth. (14) And it shall come to pass, when I bring a cloud over the earth, that the bow shall be seen in the cloud: (15) And I will remember my covenant, which is between me and you and every living creature of all flesh: and the waters shall no more become a flood to destroy all flesh"(Genesis 9:12-15).

If you only believe what was stated in 2 Peter 3:5, why would God destroy this Earth twice with water after He made a promise to not do this again? God loves us very much, even though we fell short in glory from the temptation of Satan. Our Lord gave us another chance by serving a purpose in return, with His promises and covenants of those who obey. He existed and created us for His glory and pleasure. We must be able to trust Him and ourselves to serve His purpose. His creations began from a dateless time that are never completely destroyed, but either recycled or reborn. He had given power to His mortal and immortal creations to recycle or rebirth themselves.

Chapter 5

GOD'S BIBLICAL PROMISES

Chapter 4 discussed the reasons of our purposes, how to discover them, and the possible event of reincarnation. After all that you have read in chapter 4, you want to know how can you apply your purposes with understanding from the promises of God's word. Well, this chapter will give you a list of verses abstracted from the bible. This list will provide an abstracted verse that represents a certain area in your life where you may need it the most. This is why God strongly encourages us to READ the bible, because EVERY challenge or event that will be faced in life is backed by a corresponding verse of promises and covenants. Each verse listed will have the book name, chapter, and verse that relates to common problems that we face everyday.

Prayer is important to God, but just praying without reading the bible will eventually weaken faith and knowledge of God. Above all things in a man's life, God wants him to prosper and obtain WISDOM. Without wisdom, man can lose all that he worked so hard for. This is one of the most important and powerful tools that man need for growth in prosperity and survival. Prayer without wisdom is like faith without works, here's a verse that supports how important wisdom is to God after Solomon prayed for understanding:(9)"Give therefore thy servant an understanding heart to judge they people, that I may discern between good and bad: for who is able to judge this thy so great a people? (10)And the speech pleased the Lord, that Solomon had asked this thing. (11) And God said unto him, because thou hast asked this thing, and hast not asked riches for thyself, nor hast asked the life of thine enemies; but hast ASKED FOR THYSELF UNDERSTANDING to discern judgment; (12) Behold, I have done according to thy words: lo, I have given thee a wise and an understanding heart; so that there was none like thee before thee, neither after thee shall any arise like unto thee. (13) And I have also given thee that which thou hast not asked, both riches, and honour: so that there shall not be any among the kings like unto thee all thy days"(1 Kings 3:9-13). Also, the entire Book of Proverbs speaks how important wisdom and understanding is.

God provided man with a bible as a guidance tool for life survival and success. The biggest mistake that religious followers make is that they only listen to what their religious leader says without reading what the religion is all about. There are many preachers or ministers that say or interpret a few things that are not in the religion's bible or holy book, that they even fail to read sometimes. This book is referenced from a Christian bible. Christian bibles have many parables that may have figurative speeches, or interpretations that may need to be studied and researched before it can be understood. The list of verses that are about to be provided may need a deeper understanding with self-research, but they will be explained in lament terms as much as possible from a Christian bible only. Again, as mentioned through out this book, these verses that are about to be presented are not to persuade a belief or religion of any sort; it is only introducing verses that could guide a novice Christian, a person who is interested in becoming one, or a person who simply wants a deeper understanding of God. My deep sincere apology goes out to non-believers who may had already read the book this far and still remain firm in their belief system. Some verses may be offensive to even some whom that are believers of God, but ALL verses are STRICTLY from a Christian bible.

The verses will be from the words of God and Jesus that could help in every area of life from personal habits to success. Some verses may seem superficial for some people, but there are many mysteries out there that are not religiously involved or motivated, and yet it's real. The purpose of the verses that are about to be presented is to be able to understand what God expects from us, and what we should expect from Him. If you love and believe in your parents, it's the same scenario from the words they taught and promised you with expectations from both parties. Now that you have the understanding of what is about to be presented, I hope that you are ready to better yourself and the relationship of your Maker. Another word of caution, as mentioned earlier, no matter how much you pray or believe, if it's only meant for you it will happen. You may apply these verses in your life, but they will work only if something is meant for you. This is the mistake that many fail in their belief, it's ok to believe, but make sure that you have already felt the desire or other intuitive feeling in your heart of what God had initially given you.

Every time you think about praying, think about Jesus of how much he prayed in Gethsemane, and God still lead His son's purpose to the cross. However, there may be things that you didn't pray for and God gave it to you anyway, like in the case of Solomon's prayer. The purpose of prayer is to talk to God for reassurance of the promises of His word, though prayers may not be answered frequently. Likewise, you may request to others whom may not answer, because they either wasn't ready to help you, or just wasn't able to do so at an inappropriate time. While praying you should recite God the promise that you're praying about. So here are the verses of God's expectations, promises, and covenants:

VERSES OF GOD'S PROMISES:

WHEN IN DEBT: "…and thou shalt lend unto many nations, and thou shalt not borrow…(13)And the Lord shall make thee the head, and not the tail…" (Deut. 12-13) …."for it is He that giveth thee power to get wealth…." (Deut. 8:18).

PROMISE OF HEALING: "And the Lord will take away from thee all sickness…."(Deut. 7:15).

TO KNOW THE POWER OF LOVE: "…He that hateth his brother is in darkness, and walketh in darkness, and knoweth not whither he goeth, because that darkness hath blinded his eyes"(1 John 2:11).

TO LEARN FORGIVENESS: "….If thy brother trespass against thee, rebuke him; and IF he repent, forgive him" (Luke 17:3).

WHEN DEPRESSED: "The righteous cry, and the Lord heareth, and delivered them out of all their troubles"…
(Psalm 34:17). "…Go your way, eat the fat, and drink the sweet, and send portions unto them for whom nothing is prepared: for this day is holy unto our Lord: neither be ye sorry…"(Nehemiah 8:10).

HAVING ANXIETY: "Take therefore no thought for the morrow: for the morrow shall take thought for the things of itself…."(Matthew 6:34).

ENCOURAGEMENT: "Be strong and of a good courage, fear not, nor be afraid of them: for the Lord thy God, He it is that doth go with thee; He will not fail thee, nor forsake thee"(Deut. 31:6).

FOR GUIDANCE and FINDING A PURPOSE: "For I know the thoughts that I think toward you, saith the Lord, thoughts of peace, and not of evil, to give you an expected end"..... "Before I formed thee in the belly I knew thee....and ordained thee a prophet unto the nations"(Jeremiah 29:11 & 1:5).

LESSON ON PRAYER: "And when ye stand praying, forgive, if ye have ought against any: that your Father also which is in heaven may forgive you your trespasses" (Mark 11:25).

POWER OF WORDS: "For by thy words thou shalt be justified, and by thy words thou shalt be condemned" (Matthew 12:37). "....he shall have whatsoever he saith" (Mark 11:23).

POWER TO CAST DEMONS: "Behold, I give unto you power to tread on serpents and scorpions, and over all the power of the Enemy; and nothing shall by any means hurt you"(Luke 10:19).

WHEN IN TROUBLE: (2)"When thou passest through the waters, I will be with thee; and through the rivers, they shall not overflow thee: when thou walkest through the fire, thou shalt not be burned...(3)For I am the Lord thy God..."(Isaiah 43:2-3).

STRENGTH and MOTIVATION:"I can do all things through Christ which strengthen me"(Philippians 4:13).

SUCCESS by putting GOD FIRST: (5)"....lean not unto thine own understanding.(6) In all thy ways acknowledge Him, and He shall direct thy paths" (Proverbs 3:5-6).

TO HAVE COMPASSION: (8)"Finally, be ye all of one mind, having compassion one of another, love as brethren, be pitiful, be

courteous:(9)Not rendering evil for evil, or railing for railing....
that ye should inherit a blessing"(1 Peter 3:8-9).

WHEN LONGING for the RIGHT MATE: "And the Lord God
said, it is not good that the man should be alone; I will make him
an help meet for him"(Genesis 2:18).

TO REQUEST anything YOU NEED:
"...My God shall supply all your need according to His riches in
glory by Christ Jesus"(Philippians 4:19).

TO BE TREATED the way you WANT TO BE TREATED:
"Therefore all things whatsoever ye would that men should
do to you, do ye even so to them: for this is the law and the
prophets"(Matthew 7:12). Other words, if you treat someone
negatively, expect the same in return. If you want love and
respect, you must give it for it to be returned to you. Though
we should not return the evil that was done to us, Jesus is just
saying that if you treat someone disrespectful in anyway, don't
cry wolf when someone has done the same to you. As Jesus
stated, this is the law, which is the law of the universe of what
we call Murphy's Law.

These are all the verses that God promised to get you through
life to serve His purpose. The web site below is a link to more
sources of information needed for a particular prayer or guidance
tools for understanding challenges that are faced everyday.
http://www.topbibleverses.com/ . For various additional biblical
verses that match your needs of prayer and guidance. Also, there
is another web source that has vast information on different
translations on well over 20 bibles from different languages. If
it's a verse that you can't quite understand this web site has all the
books of the bible listed. There are 3 small drop-down selections
that has the books' name, chapter, and verse that can be selected
from each box to the top left of web page. Whatever book you
select, an explanation is given from commentaries. This web

site so universal, you may need to view it for a moment before attempting to use it! Please do yourself a favor and do your own virtual tour of the site, it's very user friendly though. Here is the web address: http://bible.cc/genesis/1-1.htm .

OVERVIEW OF THE VERSES

WHEN YOU ARE IN DEBT: Have you ever wondered that even after you've paid your tithe, why God still hasn't blessed you? What have you done to not deserve the blessing? If you're barely able to afford to feed your family, not keeping a roof over their head by attempting to pay a tithe, you are practicing against God's principles, here is a verse to support this fact: "But if any provide not for his own, and specially for those of his own house, he hath denied the faith, and is worse than an infidel"(1 Timothy 5:8); and:(13)"But when thou makest a feast, call the poor, the maimed, the lame, the blind:(14)And thou shalt be blessed; FOR THEY CANNOT recompense thee..."(Luke 14:12-14). Being in debt and suffering from other issues is considered a curse, because you have disobeyed God's law in your issue. This is why READING the bible is important. God doesn't want to hear excuses. Please visit this website on the laws of tithing, be prepared, this may surprise you:http://www.tithingrusskelly.com/id23.html . Many are in debt also because, it could be other habits of how money is spent unwisely. Here are several verses on money management:

For budgeting: Leviticus 9:13 and Deut. 25:13-15.
For fair negotiations: Proverbs 22:16.
Give: Luke 6:38, Acts 20:35 and Matthew 6:3-4
Lend honestly: Luke 6:35 and Matthew 5:42
Saving money: 1 Cor. 16:2
Don't overwork: Psalms 127:2

WHEN YOU ARE SICK: we get an illness, because it was either something that we done or something that was out of our control. All you can do is pray and believe by: telling God that you believe that it can be done through Your promise of Your word. Either use the verse listed above or use another one on healing, by reciting to God reminding Him that this is what You said. You MUST read the entire verse while in prayer with all of your soul and strength to Him! Prayers are answered on different time lengths. If the healing prayer wasn't answered, do not despair in anger; for some reason, it was meant for you to be this way to allow others to appreciate their well-being.

POWER OF LOVE: many don't realize how powerful love can be. Hate brings illness to your body, and it's not good for the soul either. So, if you thinking that you have an unanswered prayer over your illness or other issue, consider in asking God why. Sooner or later, God will guide or reveal to you somehow of what you could be doing wrong. Here is a verse that proves the level of your love or hate towards another can indeed effect your body: "A sound heart is the life of the flesh: but envy the rottenness of the bones"(Proverbs 14:30); and: "A merry heart doeth good like a medicine: but a broken spirit drieth the bones"(Proverbs 17:22). Visit this website that describes each spiritual rooted disease and what causes them: http://www.mindsync.com/lam/root.htm .

BE ABLE TO FORGIVE: true love doesn't operate or exist without being able to forgive. We all had someone that done something bad to us, that sometimes are beyond our imagination, and letting it go can be difficult, but forgiveness should be done. However, there is an exception to this rule if the offender shows no remorse or offered repentance to you: as if he/she was glad that this offense was done to you. As stated in Luke 17:3, the keywords are 'if he repents', then you should forgive that person. Otherwise, rebuke the person, which is the same as: harsh criticizing, or to convey one's disapproval of something. Likewise, when we do something against God and not asking for forgiveness can be dangerous to you! He will surely have His vengeance upon you that you wished never had happened! So, if a person doesn't offer repentance to you, rebuke him/her, let it go, stay away, and put it in God's hands. As He reminds us, that vengeance is His, and by taking matters in your hands is a dangerous tactic that leads into trouble.

WHEN HAVING DEPRESSION OR ANXIETY: don't despair just because something didn't happened the way you thought it would. God knows about everything you suppose to do, and what you suppose to have that will fit your purpose. If something went wrong, share it, don't withhold it. Read James 5:16 in regards to sharing your faults to others, it worked for me!

ENCOURAGEMENT: the greatest way to find encouragement is to share problems with a good, trusted friend or family member. If you hold every problem inside of you, how can you get encouragement? No one knows your problem, and if the problem is unknown to them, how can they give you the wisdom and courage to solve it? Read Ecclesiastes 4:9-10.

FOR GUIDANCE OF FINDING A PURPOSE: finding your predestined purpose can be one of the most difficult tasks of your life. Whether you pray for it or not, your purpose will be served. Please read the Book of Jonah, it's a rather small book in the bible. This book is an example of how when a person tries to go into a different direction, other than what their heart tells them(God's speech), their purpose will be served one way or the other . As mentioned in chapters 3 & 4, Jesus tried to avoid going to the cross by prayer, and God giving you the right spirit and time to serve His purpose will be for Him.

PRAYER AND THE POWER OF WORDS: when in prayer remember to thank God for everything you have, those who need forgiveness, and those who need prayer before praying for your needs. Just praying for yourself is considered a weak prayer to God. .... "pray for one another, that ye may be healed. The effectual fervent prayer of a righteous man availeth much"(James 5:16).

God gave us power through our words, our words are like living beings that controls us. "Death and life are in the power of the tongue..."(Proverbs 18:21). Just as Jesus spoke of the power given to cast out demons in Luke 10:19.

WHEN TROUBLES COME: troubles come from mistakes we made, or they come from something that was out of our control. "All things come alike to all: there is one event to the righteous, and to the wicked; to the good and to the clean, and to the unclean..."(Eccl. 9:2). Many times, God allows trouble to test our faith and strength on Earth, just as we were tested in Heaven before Satan's fall. By the time God returns for us, we will surely be ready to leave this Earth of trials from Satan's wrath against us, and will more than likely be slow of being deceived again.

TO ACHIEVE STRENGTH AND MOTIVATION: the best way to get strength and motivation to carry on, is to be with others you know who will provide that to you. "Let another man praise thee, and not thine own mouth: a stranger, and not thine own lips"(Proverbs 27:2). Because if another sees that you can do this, this is telling you that you have more than you thought, which renders success. People rarely think that they have the power to bless another by using positive words, just as we bless the Lord with praises in His name. Read Psalms 135:19-21 and Luke 6:28.

TO HAVE COMPASSION: if you want compassion, you must return it to someone else who needs it. You may feel that some may not deserve compassion, and others may feel the same way about you. We all make mistakes that could be either be caused by mental or physical weaknesses that should be overlooked. Even if you are a highly intelligent person who rarely makes mistakes, you still would like compassion from someone if you make a mistake eventually. No matter how many or how little mistakes you've made, you made them, that's the bottom line. All you need is one small or big mistake to change your or another's life. You may not see instant results after offering compassion, but eventually from Murphy's Law it will be returned! So, treat another as the way you would like to be treated.

TO HAVE A COMPANION: there is someone for everybody. However, companionship may come sooner or later to some. If in doubt, remember Philippians 4:19. Include this scripture in your prayers to remind God that you read His bible, and know what to expect from His promises. Just as, after doing your homework, your parents will reward you with something of a promise once you graduate. God knows what He promised from every verse in the bible, but He just wants you to read it and recite it to Him, to present your knowledge and wisdom, which is VERY important to God. You wouldn't want incapable employees working for you, just as God doesn't want unwise followers to serve His purposes. He wants you as His spiritual companion to serve a purpose as a team.

Of all the overviews from each of God's promises, having the power of love is the most important: love conquers all. Your measurement of love affects your well-being, and how far you will go in life. Showing love, compassion, and understanding to others, will greatly increase your success. Having the right attitude of passion and respect can reduce much stress in your life, verses of having a negative attitude without passion. Satan wants you to be mad, negative, without love and compassion, because these qualities distracts your divine purpose that can cause many mistakes. When you are distracted by stress, negativity, and hate, this cause bad hormones, which affects your mood and concentration to control you to the point of a downward slope. You will need something like great strength of some sort to help you elevate that slope again. Sometimes it's achievable, but with harsh experiences of lessons learned.

Conclusion

God existed as a self-propelled being that no one knows how. As His appearance begins, additional matter that exists in us appeared as well. He claims that "there is no one before or after Me", and the mystery of Him will be solved. After His existence was completed, God wanted to create other beings that were celestial and terrestrial. The celestial beings were created first, which were the angels, planets, and stars. Once all the celestial beings were in order, God gave them assignments to care and watch over the created terrestrials on Earth. It was very pleasing to God when He created the terrestrials: so that praises, prayers, and burnt sacrifices can ascend to Him. Whichever type of offering or sacrifice that comes from the Earth, whether it's a sacrificial, praise, prayer, or burnt offerings from candles and incense, this pleases the Lord. He knows that heavenly beings can only offer so much. They can offer prayer and praises, but not sacrifices of flesh and blood.

This is why God created the first terrestrial man and eventually His mortal son Jesus, to enable the value of offering of blood. However, He created man first to offer sacrifices to strengthen man's love and understanding the principles in sacrificing. By the time Jesus came and died, man knew what agony God went through while His Son was dying on the cross. Without respecting and believing in that, there is no place for man in Heaven. Because God knows that whatever man refuse to believe, it usually involves a level of hatred. Parents, just think for a moment after telling your child that you don't believe that they can do this or that, what goes through your mind? Think about one of the characteristics of love, which doesn't condemn or cast down another. When you tell your children negative things, what is your true love towards them? If you really love your child, you would find the smallest positive character in them and use it to tell them: "I believe in you, that you can do anything if it meant to happen for you!" What about telling yourself that you love yourself, but not believe in yourself at the same time? Kind of an odd concept, right? Without believing in yourself, shows a sign of dissatisfaction or discontentment within yourself. Whatever or whomever you love, you would put all of your belief in it or them, if the love is true. God wants you to have the same attitude and belief in Him and His son Jesus, because we are a reflection of Him in likeness. Think about a mirror for a moment and stare at yourself in it. What you see is your reflection that can't come towards you, but still it's you! Just as the Earth and its inhabitants are reflections of Heaven, without the Earth being able to be in certain parts of Heaven, but where it belongs.

There are verses that describe similar things that are in Heaven and on Earth as well, which indicates that the Earth and its elements are a reflection of Heaven: "And the twelve *gates* were twelve *pearls*....and the *street* of the *city* was pure *gold*, as it were transparent glass"(Rev. 21:21); ....(18)"And it was made with cherubims and *palm trees*, so that a palm tree was between a cherub and a cherub; and every cherub had two faces; ...(22)"The altar of *wood* was three cubits high, and the length thereof two cubits; and the corners thereof, were of wood: and He said unto me, this IS THE *TABLE* THAT IS BEFORE THE LORD"(Ezekiel 41:18 & 22). There are reflective events and beings that both appear in Heaven and on Earth. These 2 books of the bible are enough to convince the reflections that are between Heaven and Earth are real. To get a deeper insight of the visions between the 2 prophets, read both books above. If you don't believe the prophets, research on near-death experiences. God had prepared the heavens for all of us, but we must make a choice to where we should go, and we were created in His image and likeness to know good and evil to make those choices.

Evil was created from a result that happened in Heaven between God, Satan, and us. Satan fell because he wanted to take over us and Heaven to overthrow God, but Satan's plans didn't work out. We listened and believed Satan while in Heaven like Adam and Eve did on Earth. However, God gave us another chance by allowing us to incarnate (our fall from grace) for reconciliation. God had also given Adam and Eve a chance, otherwise it seemed that they would have died instantly after their disobedience that changed everything. They were just the reflections of what happened in Heaven before they were created. Before the fruit was bitten, Satan's fall didn't cause mortality. While the battle was won in Heaven over Satan, the battle between Satan, Adam and Eve were lost until God stepped in and cursed Satan. Evil brought in mortality for sacrifice of sins, which is assigned by the Spirit of death that will be swallowed up at the end of time: Isaiah 25:8. There are spirits that control the evil events, from the Spirit of fear(2Tim.1:7), to the Spirit of whordoms (Hosea 4:12).

Though these spirits are roaming the Earth, Jesus was sent here to help us conquer them by our freewill and power. As mentioned in chapter 3, Jesus gave us the power to cast out evil spirits. He was sent to provide us faith and strength to fight off the Devil and his demons. It's wonderful that Jesus didn't just come to Earth to die for us, but to also bless us by giving a part of His power for anything that comes against us. We may not see miracles happen everyday or as obvious like the ones in the Old Testament, but miracles still occur today in the name of Jesus: take all your troubles to Him, Amen.

REFERENCES:

The Holy Bible, KJV: Thomas Nelson, Inc. copyright© 1977, 1984, and 2001

http://annourbis.com/myths-legends/22381-8_zeus_11_jupiter.html . origin of the god Zeus cited on page: 41

http://2divineways.com/stars/information_on_stars.htm Information on stars; cited on page: 43

www.angelfire.com/mi/dinosaurs/lucifer.html Satan as Lucifer; cited on page: 51

www.heavenawaits.wordpress.com/satan-is-king-of-tyre/ . About Satan as King of Tyre; cited on page: 51

http://www.learnthebible.org/king-lemuel.html . About King Lemuel; cited on page: 54

www.cbn.com/media/index.aspx?s=/vod/GW91 . Video of a miraculously healed heart transplant patient. Cited on page: 96

http://www.popularmechanics.com/science/health/forensics/1282186 . What Jesus looked like? Cited on page: 108

http://www.religioustolerance.org/chr_jcfa.htm . Shroud of Turin, and Jesus' hair described as "wooly".

Steward, M. Original Black Jews of Israel; cited on page: 108

http://www.stewartsynopsis.com/Isreal.htm
copyright 2002-2011; cited on page: 109

http://www.livestrong.com/article/72522-effects-depression-body/ . copyright 2011, Demand Media
How depression effects body. Cited on page: 117

www.reduce-your-anxiety.com/index.html . Anxiety:Cited on page: 118

http://www.unification.net/dp73/dp73-1-3.html . example of last days. Cited on page: 134

http://www.sacred-texts.com/chr/tbr/tbr094.htm "new heaven and new earth"; cited on page: 134

Clark, Mark. http://godskingdomfirst.org/GapTheory.htm . gap theory; cited on page: 134

http://www.topbibleverses.com/ . Biblical verse category.
Copyright 2010, Real. Powerful. Timeless. Cited on page: 143

http://bible.cc/genesis/1-1.htm . Biblos. Copyright 2004-2011.
Universal biblical site; cited on page: 143

http://www.tithing-russkelly.com/id23.html . Tithing
Cited on page: 144

http://www.mindsync.com/lam/root.htm . Spiritually Rooted Diseases. Life Application Ministries. Cited on page: 146

www.endtimeprophecy.net/Articles/satan-02.html . Satan's location in Tyrus. Cited on page: 51

Author Contact information:
If you have any questions, concerns, or comments,
please feel free to contact me at: ourpurposes@aol.com

If you want to DONATE
please use Pay Pal with the email address provided.